THE CULTURAL MIND

Drawing attention to the pivotal ideas associated with "the science of the cultural mind," this book centers on the idea that the human mind should be considered a sociocultural, rather than a natural or biological, phenomenon. Far from being purely theoretical, the science of the cultural mind has direct, practical implications for areas such as child development, the assessment of learning processes, and future-oriented education. The chapters are organized around five pivotal ideas and their applications, including mediated learning, symbolic tools, and leading activity. The book also provides a systematic review of the Vygotskian theory and its contemporary implications in cognitive development. Written in an accessible and engaging style, this book contains examples of practical applications of the sociocultural theory of learning that will benefit students, researchers, and practitioners in child development, educational psychology, culture studies, and education.

ALEX KOZULIN is Professor and Head of the Masters of Education Program in Special Education at Achva Academic College, Israel, and the Academic Director of International Research and Training at the Feuerstein Institute, Israel. He is one of the major international experts in Vygotsky's sociocultural theory and the theory of mediated learning.

T0371539

THE CULTURAL MIND

The Sociocultural Theory of Learning

ALEX KOZULIN

Achva Academic College and the Feuerstein Institute

CAMBRIDGE
UNIVERSITY PRESS

Shaftesbury Road, Cambridge CB2 8EA, United Kingdom

One Liberty Plaza, 20th Floor, New York, NY 10006, USA

477 Williamstown Road, Port Melbourne, VIC 3207, Australia

314–321, 3rd Floor, Plot 3, Splendor Forum, Jasola District Centre,
New Delhi – 110025, India

103 Penang Road, #05–06/07, Visioncrest Commercial, Singapore 238467

Cambridge University Press is part of Cambridge University Press & Assessment,
a department of the University of Cambridge.

We share the University's mission to contribute to society through the pursuit of
education, learning and research at the highest international levels of excellence.

www.cambridge.org
Information on this title: www.cambridge.org/9781009327084

DOI: 10.1017/9781009327060

© Alex Kozulin 2024

This publication is in copyright. Subject to statutory exception and to the provisions
of relevant collective licensing agreements, no reproduction of any part may take
place without the written permission of Cambridge University Press & Assessment.

First published 2024

A catalogue record for this publication is available from the British Library

A Cataloging-in-Publication data record for this book is available from the Library of Congress

ISBN 978-1-009-32708-4 Hardback
ISBN 978-1-009-32704-6 Paperback

Cambridge University Press & Assessment has no responsibility for the persistence
or accuracy of URLs for external or third-party internet websites referred to in this
publication and does not guarantee that any content on such websites is, or will
remain, accurate or appropriate.

Contents

Figures, Tables, and Boxes

Figures

Tables

Boxes

Introduction
The Science of the Cultural Mind

The main objective of this book is to draw the readers' attention to some pivotal ideas of what one may call "the science of the cultural mind." Some of these ideas were first introduced almost a century ago, but they still require clarification and identification of their yet unrealized potential. The main idea, of course, is that the human mind and first of all cognition and learning should be considered a sociocultural, rather than a natural or biological, phenomenon. There are many biological and behavioral functions shared by human beings and animals, but the goal of the science of the cultural mind is to explore only the specifically human aspects of the human mind. These exclusively human functions are intimately related to the social and cultural world which constitutes the "natural" environment of human beings.

Far from being only theoretical, the science of the cultural mind has direct practical implications for such areas as child development, new approaches to the assessment of cognitive and learning processes, and future-oriented education. The book is organized around five pivotal ideas and their applications: The idea of human *mediation* (Chapter 1), the concept of *symbolic tools* and their impact on human mental functions (Chapter 2), the idea of *leading activities* that provides a new perspective on the periods of child development (Chapter 3), the concept of *learning potential* and the methods of its assessment (Chapter 4), and the idea of *cognitive education* as a vehicle of the more efficient development of students' conceptual thinking (Chapter 5).

Mediation. This concept helps us to explain the interaction between human beings and their environments. These interactions are rarely immediate, though it is often tempting to see them in this way. We propose to check beyond the apparent immediacy of human interaction with the environment and discover different types of mediators. Some of these mediators are material: The fire mediates between us and the food we eat; glasses mediate between our visual system and distant objects that we would like to see; mechanical tools mediate between our hands and a material that we would like to shape according to our needs, and so on. There is no end of knowledge accumulated about these material mediators. However, one question that was posed almost a century ago remains mainly unanswered: How do these material mediators influence our thinking? Buildings, clothes, tools, furniture, and vehicles themselves are material, and their interaction with us is also mainly material (providing shelter and helping to create useful goods, transportation, etc.), but it appears that our mind is not immune to the influence of these material mediators. The question is how this influence is taking place. A hint: These mediators are shaped by our cultures, so it is not their physical but rather their cultural aspect that impacts our cultural mind.

The second class of mediators includes symbolic mediators, such as signs, symbols, icons, texts, pictures, formulae, graphs, maps, and diagrams. It is impossible to imagine any culture without at least some of these mediators. Thousands of works are written about them in different specialized areas such as literary theory (about texts), art history (pictures), mathematics (formulae), and musicology (musical notations). In many of these fields, only one representational aspect of symbols is discussed. Symbols, however, not only represent objects, processes, and events but also mediate between the world and the human mind and in the process impact the way our cognitive processes are shaped. Just imagine the difference between the experience of orienting oneself in a new city being armed with such a symbolic mediator as a map or having to rely on direct vision and hearing alone. The use of a map not only changes our perception of the city but also changes the way we think about the space and our place in it. In the theory of the cultural mind, symbolic mediators play a very important role because the study of these mediators helps us to understand how our natural functions of perception, memory, and problem-solving become transformed into cultural mental functions corresponding to the symbolic tools available to us.

The third class of mediators is people. For example, mothers by and large serve as reliable mediators between their young children and the environment. Mothers select objects and events to which children are exposed, sometimes emphasize or on the contrary downplay certain aspects of the exposure, interpret environmental events to children, prevent children from entering into dangerous situations, etc. Of course, parents are not the only human mediators: Teachers and other mentors take over some of the functions of human mediators by guiding children through the cultural environment of formal and informal learning. The examination of the role of human mediators helps us to understand better such phenomena as learning deprivation, developmental difficulties, and alienation.

The fourth class of mediators is activities. Of course, activities do not exist without some material, symbolic, and human mediators, and yet activities cannot be reduced to any one of the previous types of mediators. Just imagine any ritual, even such an ordinary one as a weekend evening dinner for the entire family. The dinner ritual includes such material mediators as furniture, tools, and food; it may also have some symbolic objects and recitation of texts. Adults play an important role as mediators to the children participating in the dinner, and beyond all of this there is a "weekend dinner" as a form of collective activity that cannot be reduced to any of the previously mentioned mediators. Daily or festive rituals, of course, constitute just one type of activity. Formal education, on the one hand, and professional work, on the other, are among the main forms of activity in technologically developed societies. The question is how these activities impact the development of the human cultural mind. For example, how does such an activity as formal learning shape the type of learning abilities appropriated by the students? On the other hand, how does the activity of professional work impact our cognition?

While not many people would question the importance of mediation for human development, the majority of research methodologies still assume that human cognition can be investigated by registering a direct response of a person to a task provided by the researchers. For example, in a study of a child's orientation in space, it is tacitly assumed that this ability is a product of maturation on the one hand and the child's own experience on the other. As a result, typical research in this area would check only children's spontaneously acquired orientation abilities. What, however, about first providing children with relevant mediation via symbolic tools, human mediation, or specific activities relevant to spatial orientation and only then checking their orientation in space? Unfortunately, such an approach, which is consistent with the principles of the science of the cultural mind, rarely appears in the research literature. In other words, though no one would deny that human beings are cultural beings, they are still investigated as if they are only natural beings.

Symbolic tools. The already-mentioned concept of symbolic mediation is further elaborated in Chapter 2. There we focus on the following sequence of steps leading from symbolic mediators to the development of human thinking. First of all, it should be acknowledged that cultures differ in the kind of symbolic mediators available to them. In addition, even within the same culture, some ethnic or socioeconomic subgroups are exposed to a different range of symbolic mediators than other subgroups. Not all children (or adults) in a given subgroup have equal success in the acquisition of certain symbolic mediators. This process depends, of course, on the skills and motivation of human mediators: first of all parents and teachers, who are expected to make these symbolic mediators available to children.

The next step is an actual acquisition of symbolic mediators as symbolic tools. A better understanding of this process requires a more detailed elaboration of the notion of the systems of symbols (graphic, pictorial, verbal, schematic, etc.), on the one hand, and the distinction between symbolic tools and material tools, on the other. Too often symbolic tools are presented to the learners (children and adults) as a part of the content material. As a result, only the representational role of symbols is revealed, while their instrumental role remains obscure. There is no doubt that symbols represent objects and processes, but their role is much wider. For example, if such a symbolic tool as a data table "represents" something, this something definitely is not the content that appears in the table. What the table "represents" is a particular way of organizing and thinking about any type of data. If so, then it is more relevant to discuss tables, graphs, and other symbols as potential tools. It is in the instrumental action, in their ability to shape, organize, and change information, that these symbols demonstrate their real power. On the individual level, the learning process moves from the acquisition of a data table as an external symbol to the realization of its instrumental function as an external symbolic tool and further to the internalization and transformation of this symbolic tool into the inner cognitive tool. One example of such a process is first learning how to use a clock as an external symbolic tool for telling the time and then internalizing and transforming this tool into an inner cognitive tool that allows perceiving time as divided into twenty-four-hour units.

The process of internalization of symbolic tools leads to the development of higher mental functions. Here we confront a serious terminology problem because cognitive specialists tend to use the same terms, such as "memory" or "attention," for both direct memorization and spontaneous attention and complex mental functions dependent on symbolic systems such as literacy and numeracy. It would be more appropriate to differentiate terminologically such basic cognitive functions as "direct memory" and the higher mental function of "mediated memory." The same distinction has to be made regarding other functions as well, such as direct perception vs. mediated perception, direct attention vs. mediated attention, and so on.

The concept of symbolic tools helps us to clarify numerous issues in three areas: Cross-cultural differences in cognition, higher mental processes of children and adults, and formal education understood as a system based on the learners' acquisition and internalization of symbolic tools. Cross-cultural differences that are often presented in terms of the average IQ scores of ethnic or cultural groups acquire new meaning when differences in symbolic tools available to various groups are taken into account. Moreover, the process of acculturation to a new environment associated with migration can be operationalized, at least in part, as a process of acquisition and mastery of the new system of symbolic tools.

As mentioned earlier, the distinction between more basic cognitive processes and mediated higher mental functions allows us to clarify some issues related to the disparity between the abilities identified with the help of tests probing basic cognitive processes and abilities revealed in more complex tasks that require higher mental functions. The case in point is children with relatively weak direct perception, memory, and attention, some of whom manage to achieve remarkable results through the acquisition and implementation of symbolic tools leading to the development of higher mental functions stronger than those of their peers. The opposite situation is with children who demonstrate very good results with the tasks that require direct perception, memory, and attention, but then fall behind because more complex tasks require mediated, rather than direct, mental functions.

This point naturally leads to the third area of application of the concept of symbolic tools: formal education. Despite the cognitive reorientation of contemporary education that lists the development of learning strategies and cognitive skills among the main objectives of the educational process, the role of symbolic tools remains insufficiently elaborated. Symbolic tools that permeate school learning – tables, graphs, diagrams, plans, and maps – often appear as an integral part of the content material. As a result, students perceive them as a part of a specific material rather than tools whose role is to organize this material. The role of symbols as active cognitive tools thus remains underappreciated by the learners. An additional problem stems from the fact that when the educational role of symbolic tools is discussed this is usually done in a narrow disciplinary framework. In the absence of a common theoretical basis, symbolic tools become "assigned" to a particular curricular area. For example, the use of maps remains confined to geography, while the use of tables and graphs is limited to mathematics and physics. We propose a way for positioning symbolic tools at the center of the educational process, facilitating in this way the more efficient development of the learners' higher mental functions.

Leading activities. As mentioned earlier, one of the forms of mediation is mediation via specially organized activities. In the course of their development children become engaged in different age-appropriate activities. Though at a given age children are involved in various activities, it is still possible to argue that for each developmental period there is one leading activity. The role of a leading activity is to develop some of the core psychological functions that are most important at a given stage of child development. Unlike such popular developmental models as that of Piaget that present developmental stages as universal, the leading activities model is culturally specific. In the form presented here, it applies only to child (and adult) development in industrialized societies that have a formal educational system. The culturally specific character of the leading activities model finds its expression in presenting the developmental event as a joint action in which the child's emerging abilities (sensory, motor, cognitive, and emotional) meet the socioculturally constructed activities (different forms of play, formal learning, social group activities, work, etc.) provided by a given community. As a result of such a meeting, the child's abilities mature in the direction supported by the community while simultaneously paving the way to the child's transition to the next developmental period.

During each one of the developmental periods, the progression of the child's cognitive and interpersonal skills leads to the formation of a new motive that corresponds to the new leading activity in the next developmental period. For example, the emotional component is central during the earliest period in child development, while the manipulation of objects (toys) plays a subdominant role. Gradually, however, the object-centered joint activity with adults becomes a new motive of the child and at a certain moment assumes the role of the leading activity while the emotional contact becomes subdominant. Similarly, the leading activity of object-centered play gradually prepares the child for the transition to sociodramatic play. While during the first of these two periods, manipulation with a toy car is focal, in the second period the imaginary role of a driver becomes the main interest of the child, with a toy car relegated to the subdominant role of one of the play's physical prompts. Sociodramatic play has an important role in preparing children for formal education. On the one hand, symbolic aspects of such play enrich children's ability to assign certain meanings to objects beyond their superficial physical properties. The development of play-based imagination will pay off later via children's emerging ability to use written texts for imagining remote places, different historical periods, or unobservable physical conditions. Moreover, sociodramatic play "teaches" children how to switch from one role to another, for example, from the role of a truck driver to that of a policeman and then back. Such flexibility in switching roles will become indispensable when children enter a formal education framework and switches from the family-based role of a son or daughter to the role of a pupil.

In societies with formal education systems, the leading activity during the period approximately coinciding with elementary school age is the activity of formal learning. Formal learning as a leading activity should be distinguished from the generic form of learning. Generic learning is ubiquitous at every stage of child (and adult) development. Generic learning is an integral part of other activities, such as emotional interaction, play, and work. However, according to the leading activity model, only during the period of formal education does learning becomes a leading activity. The specificity of this period is determined by the fact that the goal of formal learning is to transform a child into a self-directed learner. The main goal of formal education is in helping the child "learn how to learn." Learning here is not a supporting element of some other activity; the products of formal learning – written essays, solved math tasks, or results of lab experiments – do not have any value in themselves but only as means for the transformation of a child into a "universal learner": a learner who can learn anything. This feature of formal learning becomes particularly relevant in the context of the fundamental uncertainty regarding the future occupations of children who started their formal education in the twenty-first century. The most valuable skill that they can acquire at school is the ability to learn something new and unpredictable. Some of the practical educational applications of this type of leading activity are discussed in Chapter 5.

Though we focus mainly on the two types of leading activity – sociodramatic play and formal learning – it is important to understand that the leading activity model assumes that formal learning does not remain the leading activity for the entire period of schooling. Already at the middle school age, the youngsters' leading activity shifts from that of formal learning to the activity of interpersonal relationships leading to the formation of the youngster's mature personality. Such a shift creates a problem for an educational system that is rather uniformly built around learning tasks while the students focus on interpersonal relationships. We discuss how more flexible forms of learning, such as projects, may utilize the students' desire for interpersonal interaction as a motor for their further scholastic development.

Learning potential. Though thousands of books have been written about learning, the concept of learning potential (LP) remains insufficiently elaborated. One of the possible reasons for such a state of affairs is the tendency to view learning only through its products. When a math or history exam is given to students it is assumed that the results of the exam will reveal the efficiency of students' previous learning. In other words, what we can see in such an exam is only the result rather than the process of learning. Moreover, such an exam provides us with relatively little information about each student's potential for learning something new. For example, one student can achieve good exam results by investing much more time in learning than another student who achieved the same result. The efficiency of the first one is thus lower than that of the second student, but this factor is "hidden" in a typical exam. The situation is even more complicated in the case of so-called intelligence tests. Some psychologists insist that properly designed intelligence test taps into the individual's innate abilities that are unrelated to his or her learning experiences. Others, however, define intelligence itself as a "general learning ability" and claim that intelligence tests provide us with a pretty accurate estimate of not only personal knowledge but also the person's learning ability. Irrespective of the definition, however, the results of intelligence tests provide information only about people's current knowledge and problem-solving skills but say little about their LP.

The situation can be changed rather radically if active learning is included as an integral element in the assessment procedure itself. This can be done in a variety of ways. For example, the LP test can be designed as a test–teach–test sequence. First, the entire test or exam is given to a person, then the assessor examines the results, identifies more salient mistakes, and then gives a teaching session focusing on the knowledge or/and skills responsible for the mistakes. After such a teaching session, an examinee is given a post-test that is parallel to the pre-test. The level of a person's LP can thus be determined by the difference between pre- and post-test scores and the change in the types of mistakes made before and after the teaching session. Another possibility is to divide the test or exam into separate questions and prepare a sequence of cues or prompts to be given after a specific mistake is made in response to each one of the questions. In the end, the examinee always reaches the correct answer because the last cue actually provides the correct solution. In this case, the examinee's LP is estimated as the opposite of the number of received cues. The fewer cues a person needs for responding correctly to the question, the higher his/her LP.

These LP assessment procedures can be used with test materials similar to those of standard cognitive tests, such as sequences of numbers or figures, matrices, and verbal or pictorial analogies. The LP assessment can also be carried out with tasks reflecting practically any curricular material: language, mathematics, history, science, and so on. Once the idea of LP assessment entered the field of the school curriculum, an interesting dialogue started between it and the following, somewhat related, assessment approaches in contemporary education: formative assessment, adaptive assessment, and response to intervention.

LP and formative assessment share a common orientation toward the future of students' learning rather than their past. While so-called summative assessment aims at taking stock of the knowledge and skills already acquired by students, formative assessment aims at providing guidance for future teaching and learning. In a sense, formative assessments can be imagined as a series of test–teach–test episodes that provide teachers with ongoing information about the effectiveness of their teaching and the responsiveness of students. The main difference between LP and formative assessments is related to their history. The concept of LP assessment originally emerged in response to dissatisfaction with static intelligence tests and only later "drifted" to the curricular areas. It is still firmly connected to its roots in psychological and developmental theories. Formative assessment in its turn emerged from the classroom practice in response to dissatisfaction with summative exams aimed at ranking students' subject achievements but providing little information for changing the course of instruction. It is difficult to discern a common theoretical basis for different formative assessments that are often created in a rather intuitive way by teachers themselves for their specific teaching needs (Greenstein, 2010).

The second form of assessment to be compared to LP is the so-called adaptive assessment. This type of assessment emerged in response to the problem of using the same test or exam with students of different performance levels. For some of the students, a given exam could be too difficult and lead to frustration; for others it could be too easy and thus fail to evaluate their true ability. The availability of computers as a medium for storing a large number of tasks and displaying them to students provided further impetus for adaptive assessment, particularly in mathematics. The adaptive assessment starts with a presentation to a student of the task of average difficulty for his or her age group. If the student fails to solve the problem, an easier task of the same type is presented. If the second, easier task is also not solved, even the simpler task is provided. After each correct solution, the student is given a more challenging task. In this way assessment via computer becomes individualized and its results provide richer information about students' problem-solving abilities. At a certain moment, adaptive assessment procedures started acquiring features that bring them closer to LP assessment. This happened when instead of simply providing the student with the easier task the computer program provided him or her with hints or cues that "matched" the mistake that has been made. In this way, the learning phase has been effectively introduced into the adaptive assessment procedure so that the students' LP could be evaluated through the type and number of cues or hints needed to solve a problem of a certain level of difficulty. Two main differences between adaptive assessment and LP are the content area and the use of computers. While LP assessments span a wide range of areas, from intelligence tests to school subject exams, so far adaptive assessments have been used almost exclusively in math teaching. Moreover, while LP assessment usually involves a human mediator, the advantage of adaptive assessments is in their computer-based nature.

Finally, the response to intervention (RTI) methodology emerged primarily in response to the need for early detection and prevention of learning disabilities in children at the beginning of formal education. Some of the sources of this methodology are more pragmatic, while others are more theoretical. The pragmatic aspect is related to the difficulty in providing all children who demonstrate some literacy or numeracy problems with professional assessments carried out by psychologists or reading/math specialists. As a result, some of the children remain without proper intervention, while others are erroneously labeled as "learning disabled." The theoretical basis of RTI is related to dissatisfaction with the so-called achievement gap definition of learning disability. The "gap" is between the school achievement expected of the child with a given level of intelligence and his or her actual low achievement. One of the problems with the "gap" definition is that it not only depends on the availability of intelligence testing of all "at-risk" children but also on the actual school failure of the child. Instead of waiting for a child to show the gap, the RTI methodology proposes to start the process of intervention as early as possible and to watch for the level of children's response to intervention. Those children who respond positively to intervention may have some learning difficulties, but they should not be labeled as disabled. Only those children who fail to respond positively to increasingly intensive and individualized forms of intervention can indeed be classified as learning disabled and be provided with appropriate special education treatment.

There is a certain affinity between RTI and LP assessment, but they are not identical. First of all, while RTI follows the teach–test–teach sequence, the LP assessment is based on the test–teach–test model. Second, RTI focuses on offering an alternative to the prevention of learning disabilities while LP has a much broader range of goals. In addition, so far the RTI approach has been applied almost exclusively in the early grades, while the LP assessment model is used with all ages. At the same time, the belief in the modifiability of cognition and learning provides a common theoretical basis for LP and RTI. Some of the RTI studies in practice include some LP assessments in their research methodology.

Cognitive education. It became almost a cliché to say that in the twenty-first century, education cannot be based on teaching specific content and skills but should focus on "learning how to learn." The question is how to translate this general philosophy into concrete learning practice. In a traditional school, the most desirable qualities of a good student were the ability to follow the model presented by the teacher, recall and perform standard operations, and remember a large amount of factual information. Exactly the same qualities would also help students to receive high scores on IQ tests and in college admission exams like the SAT. Are these qualities important? Of course they are! All of them are important, but they are also insufficient. In the past, the qualities beyond those of a "good student" were required only for a minority of high school graduates who aspired to become researchers and embark on an academic career. Scholars have never remained just "good students": They knew that constant learning of new approaches and techniques is a condition *sine qua non* of any scientific enterprise. Nowadays these "scientific" qualities seem to be required of almost every high school graduate.

There are two major proposals for handling this problem. The first of them suggests focusing on students' general cognitive and problem-solving skills which can then be applied in any content area. The second proposal is to develop cognitive strategies "inside" the curricular areas. The first approach thus calls for the addition of a new learning subject – "cognitive lessons" – while the second presupposes a rather radical reform of curricular teaching/learning that would assign cognitive goals to subject lessons.

There are two areas in which the "cognitive lessons" approach is less controversial: early childhood education and special education. Many of the cognitive activities constitute a part of the kindergarten curricula, irrespective of their theoretical orientation. After all, kindergartens are expected to support child development that requires some key cognitive functions (perception, memory, attention, problem-solving), enhancing children's language and communication, and facilitating their understanding of social and emotional behaviors. Almost the same goals, but for different age groups, are included in special education curricula. There is a wide consensus that children with special needs should be provided not only with such standard curricular subjects as reading, math, and history but also with more general cognitive and learning strategies.

The introduction of cognitive lessons into a regular elementary or high school curriculum is more controversial. The first objection is theoretical while the second is more practical and organizational. The theoretical objection stems from the fact that while the importance of general cognitive skills is well accepted, the efficiency of their transfer from cognitive education lessons to curricular learning remains elusive. In other words, if the strategy of, for example, selecting parameters for comparing two objects or processes is recognized as educationally important, the transfer of this strategy from specially designed cognitive lessons to literature, history, or math learning remains problematic. One may notice that the controversy is related to the paradox inherent in the "learning how to learn" paradigm. Within this paradigm, cognitive lessons are expected to prepare the student for confronting future, still unknown learning challenges. At the same time, the evaluation of the effectiveness of cognitive education is usually carried out by its impact on the mastery of the "old," well-known curricular material. The second objection to cognitive education is more organizational and is related to the entrenched structures of the school curriculum and teacher training. Despite having sympathy for the "learning how to learn" paradigm, school administrations are reluctant to reduce the number of language, math, or science lessons for the sake of such a relatively unknown subject as cognitive education. The professional identity of teachers is also well entrenched; everyone has some idea of what it means to be good math or history teacher, but not much is known about how to evaluate a cognitive education teacher.

As mentioned earlier, the other way of dealing with "learning how to learn" is to develop the student's cognitive strategies "inside" the curricular areas. For the sake of brevity, we call this approach "infusion," meaning the infusion of cognitive goals into curricular teaching and learning. One can distinguish theory-based "infusion" and intuitive "infusion." The theory-based infusion approach is associated with the concept of formal learning as a leading activity mentioned in Chapter 3. The key cognitive function that formal education is expected to develop in primary school students is reflection or metacognition, in other words, the ability to critically examine every task and every learning action. Imagine that the following task is given to the students: Ann has two apples more than Betty, and Betty has three apples more than Carol. How many apples do all three girls have together? Some of the students can make a simple mistake by adding two and three and responding that the girls altogether have five apples. However, some students who spontaneously developed skills of critical reasoning would respond that the problem has no correct solution "because we don't know how many apples Carol has." The goal of the cognitive infusion approach, however, is to lead students to a more detailed critical analysis. The response of these students may be something like: "There is no one correct solution to this task. However, if we assume that Carol has at least one apple, then the total number of apples cannot be less than 11." This kind of answer distinguishes what in the infusion approach is called "academic" or "scientific" concepts from so-called everyday concepts. The infusion approach proposes to revise the school curriculum and the didactics of teaching so that children early on start understanding that many of the everyday concepts do not stand the test of critical scrutiny.

There are several crucial elements in the infusion approach. First of all, students early on are taught how to analyze goals, methods, and means of learning actions of themselves and other students. This goal is associated with a mastery of presenting problem-solving actions in symbolic form. Symbolization helps children to identify the essential features of the given object or event and to dispense with those that are nonessential. Second, the students are engaged in activities that counter a spontaneous egocentric position that takes into account only one dimension or point of view. These activities include peer teaching and teaching younger children. Third, the students are taught how to evaluate the results of their actions and solutions. Instead of taking task evaluations given by teachers as "authoritative decisions," the students are taught to select parameters and construct evaluation scales for the assessment of their solutions. The infusion approach to education thus includes many of the mediational agents mentioned earlier: The approach itself is based on the concept of formal education as a leading activity, teachers are perceived as human mediators rather than providers of information, and symbolic tools are involved as instruments for the development of students' higher mental functions.

CHAPTER I

Mediation

It is tempting to see human experience as a result of a direct interaction of human beings with their environment: We look at a tree and retain its image, we hear music and memorize it, we touch some fabric (e.g., silk) and form the concept of "silkiness." In some psychological theories, such as a simplified version of Piaget's theory of child development (Kamii, 1985), the child appears as a solitary explorer who directly learns about the world and its laws. In this chapter we try to show that direct interaction with the environment constitutes just one source of our knowledge and experience; the second source is mediated interaction. Moreover, rather often what at first glance appears as direct interaction, after some analysis reveals its mediated nature. Mediated interactions depend on several types of mediators: physical, symbolic, and human. To identify the role of each one of these mediators we should start, however, by contrasting direct interaction and mediated interaction.

Direct vs. Mediated

Let us imagine the following futuristic scenario. In the future, newborn babies will find themselves in a safe and enriching environment with controlled temperature, nutrients provided automatically at the right moment, and a variety of stimuli: colors, shapes, and sounds that enrich their life experience. The only element missing in this environment is other human beings, for example, mothers and fathers. As babies grow, their environment expands, offering more and more opportunities for children to explore both natural and human-made objects such as furniture, various tools, trees, flowers, sand and pebbles, and pools of water.

What, in your opinion, would become of these children? Would they be able to develop the same motor skills as children in a "traditional" society? Would they spontaneously start to speak, and if so, in which language? Would they harm themselves by experimenting with tools or falling into a pool?

Let us now compare this futuristic scenario with more traditional situations of child development. The distinctive feature of human babies, unlike the babies of some animals, is a very long period of physical dependence. By responding to the physical needs of human babies their caregivers simultaneously provide them with the experience of mediated interactions. It is enough for a baby who wishes to touch a toy butterfly to make a gesture, and her caregiver (human mediator) will move the toy closer to her. The same mediator may also tell the baby: "Yes, this is a yellow butterfly, but see over there (points) we also have a red butterfly." By making this simple statement the caregiver brings an additional mediator, this time a symbolic one, into the scene of the child's experience. Speech and language are among the most prominent symbolic mediators; nothing in the sound "b-u-t-t-e-r-f-l-y" is connected to a plastic toy of a butterfly shape. Words are products of human culture that occupy the place between people and objects; words are probably the most powerful of all symbolic mediators. In addition to words, adults teach children to use different tools, and though the tools themselves are intended for changing objects, for example, brushing teeth, cutting an apple, or applying colors to a white sheet of paper, the use of these tools (material mediators) probably has a reciprocal impact on a child's mental abilities, such as comparison, selection, planning, or precision. Finally, when children enter kindergarten or school they not only become acquainted with new human mediators – teachers and peers – and with new symbolic tools associated with reading, writing, counting, and drawing, but they also become involved in mediation via structured activities, such as group pretended play or formal learning.

So, after some analysis we may conclude that the interaction of human beings with their environments is rarely direct; behind each one of the direct interactions usually stands a previously mediated interaction. The environment of the young child is rather tightly controlled by adults, who select, amplify, and interpret different features of this environment for children. As children grow up their understanding of the world becomes more and more mediated by symbolic tools: texts, pictures, diagrams, and formulae. These tools in their turn are acquired via different structured activities: games, formal learning, work apprenticeships, and so on. Greater attention to mediated interactions helps us to understand how a brain becomes a "human mind" in the sense of being shaped by interactions specific to human society in all their various historical and cultural forms.

Material Tools as Mediators

Probably no one would deny the importance of physical tools in contributing to what is called civilization. Material tools stand between us and the material world. Hammers and nails help us to connect several pieces of wood so that a new object, for example, a table, is created. A brush changes the appearance of objects because it "mediates" between the paint and the object to be painted. Coffee beans that go through the grinder change their size and structure and essentially become a new object: a coffee powder.

Figure 1.1 provides a schematic representation of the instrumental role of material tools. The direction is from a person toward the environment; the role of a tool is to change the environment for the benefit of a person. Research on the history of technology and in a broader sense the history of civilizations has accumulated a considerable amount of data about the development of material tools and the benefits they have brought to human society, as well as possible side effects such as dramatic ecological changes.

The history of science and technology usually follows the path from a human need to human imagination and from imagination to the development of new material tools. The human desire to fly or swim underwater ignited the creative genius of Leonardo da Vinci, who designed prototypes of flying machines and submarines (Buchanan, 2018). So, the idea of a flying machine first appeared in the mind of da Vinci and several centuries later it became actually realized as new technology. Even on a much simpler level, it is often assumed that both inventors and users of such basic tools as, for example, a knife have some preexistent cognitive abilities that help them to "match" the human need to the tool and its function. As explained by Osiurak et al. (2018), if one intends to cut a tomato, such a person is free to choose from a wide variety of tools, but the choice is nevertheless based on the match between the physical properties of the tomato and the physical properties of the tool. In other words, a person first thinks about something sharp and solid and then selects a tool that

Figure 1.1   Material tools are directed from human beings toward nature and change it to their benefit

corresponds to this mental image. So, first comes the need – "I would like to divide some object into parts" – then this need stimulates the human imagination, which creates several mental prototypes, and finally a new physical tool that helps a person to perform the desired operation (e.g., to cut a tomato) is either created or selected. In any case, human cognition is perceived as a prerequisite for the invention or selection of material tools.

It is tempting, however, to ask an opposite question: What about the possible reciprocal impact of new material tools on human thinking? Can we trace changes in human thinking to the availability of new physical tools and technologies? Though this question was posed almost a century ago, it still remains insufficiently investigated. By mentioning some early cultural anthropology studies, Vygotsky and Luria (1930/1993, p. 74) claimed: "The entire existence of an Australian aborigine depends on his boomerang, just as the entire existence of modern England depends upon her machines. Take the boomerang away from the aborigines, make him a farmer, then out of necessity he will have to completely change his life-style, his habits, his entire style of thinking, his entire nature." What is meant by this remark is that the hunting tool of aboriginals not only helps them to get food but also defines the comprehension of their environment. This early statement of Vygotsky and Luria is echoed in a more recent study by Barnham (2013) about the impact of the prehistorical transition from primitive tools (e.g., stone knife) made of one piece of material to hafted tools composed of several pieces of different materials. In a hafted knife the sharp stone part is directed, so to say, toward the environment, while the wooden handle is attuned to the properties of the human hand. From Barnham's (2013, p. 3) point of view, hafting not only improved the results of material tool use but also had some cognitive consequences: "But the real innovation that underpins hafting lies in envisaging the final form of the tool as an integrated whole, and that level of imagination was argu-ably something new in human evolution."

So, the question is to what extent the change in material mediators might trigger changes in human cognition. For example, it is popular to claim that the Industrial Revolution brought with it a radical change in every-day human behavior. Before the revolution, the invention and use of tools were confined to an intimate world of artisans' workshops. The number of artisans was limited, their tools were often individualized, and the predomi-nant form of learning was through apprenticeship. After the revolution, new and increasingly standardized tools started being used in factories that employed large numbers of workers who learned their trade in a more and more standardized way. Indeed, there is little doubt that such a change in

the world of work and material tools must have had an impact on workers' behavior and cognition. The challenge, however, is to reach beyond a
general idea of such an impact and to inquire into more specific changes in
human mental functions associated with changes in material tool action.

Let us consider the possible impact of one of the main new products
of the Industrial Revolution: the railroad. Before the revolution, the predominant means of transportation was a coach with a horse as a source of
power. The coachman had to take into account both the physical properties of the carriage and the behavior of the horse. The ability to control the
horse's behavior was extremely important, so the demands for the coachman's "social intelligence" (vis-à-vis the horse) were rather high. The carriage as a mechanical system, on the other hand, was not very complex,
so there was not much pressure on the coachman's "analytic intelligence."
The change to steam engine locomotives radically changed the type of psychological functions expected of the drivers. If before the revolution the
coachman's ability to control the performance of an animal was primary,
now this "social intelligence" became obsolete, while the need for "analytic intelligence" associated with working with the much more complex
mechanical system of the locomotive came to the forefront.

The introduction of trains as a means of transportation not only shifted
the priorities for the cognitive functions of drivers but also had a wider
psychological impact on the general population in terms of such mental functions as a perception of time and the need for precision (Kern,
2003; Ogle, 2015). As long as horse-driven coaches dominated the transportation scene, the time of travel from point A to point B was always
approximate: dependent on the performance of the horses and the quality of roads. What is probably more important, the time itself was local:
dependent on the local sunrise. For example, the local time in London
was fourteen minutes ahead of the local time in Exeter. These fourteen
minutes were probably not that important when the speed of horse-driven
coaches was slow and the journey from London to Exeter took a couple of
days. Everything changed with the introduction of the two new "tools": a
locomotive and a telegraph. Fast-moving trains made local times obsolete:
To have a railroad schedule the time at point A and point B should be the
same. The telegraph, apart from its other functions, further strengthened
the requirement for time precision. Messages sent from point A to point
B traveled faster than trains and were able to inform the public about possible delays. So, in fewer than 100 years the perception of time, at least
in Britain, changed radically from local and approximate to standardized
(Greenwich Mean Time) and precise.

It remains to be the task of historical psychology to investigate to what extent the change in material tools actually promoted the development of specific mental functions, for example, temporal precision, or whether these mental abilities were always present in the human mind but simply unrequested. It is possible that the emergence of new material tools simply activated these abilities or changed mental priorities. We return to this question when discussing symbolic tools in Chapter 2, but meanwhile let us focus on a more recent impact of technology on human cognitive functions.

The technology in question is the wheelchair. Quite a lot is written about the accessibility of public places by wheelchair users but very little about the possible impact of wheelchair use on spatial orientation and other cognitive functions. In this respect, an "experiment" conducted by Sophia Bannert (2013) is very instructive. Bannert, a young architect and city planner, decided to spend a day as a wheelchair user in the British city of Lincoln. The gist of her wheelchair experience points to a radical change in both perception and orientation in space prompted by the use of this tool. For example, the rarely used perceptual function of "zooming in" on environmental details became very important: "Never before had I seen the streetscape in such meticulous detail. Tiny height differences such as curbs and grooves between cobbles become mountains, cruelly halting progress and making small advances, exhausting." The "map" of such familiar objects as a supermarket became different. If before stairs were associated with an entrance to the building while their properties (height, width) were not very important, now the entrance turned out to be at the back of the building and the incline of the ramp is its most important feature: "I make my way to a ramp situated at the back entrance of a supermarket, to buy lunch. After several attempts with different approaches; I still can't heave myself up the ramp. The incline is too steep."

The function of spatial planning previously associated only with unfamiliar environments now became crucial for such a trivial activity as drinking a cup of coffee. The coffee shop counter attuned to the height of a standing person became difficult to reach for a wheelchair user because it was now above her head: "Visiting a well-known coffee chain, I soon unraveled a domino effect of obstructions which hadn't been anticipated. With the counter being high above my head, reaching for a scalding hot drink proves just as tricky as holding it whilst maneuvering a wheelchair with both arms."

In other words, the wheelchair as a mobility tool has clear cognitive consequences for its user. Now let us imagine the entire range of mobility situations, from the condition when no tool is available at all to the use of the most advanced electric wheelchair. For a person who does not have any mobility tool and is thus confined to his or her room, the whole range of mental functions (orientation in space and time, planning, self-image, etc.) will be very different from those of a person who has such a basic mobility tool as crutches. The "world with crutches," however, is not the "world with a wheelchair."

Thinking about balance is crucial for users of crutches while it is almost nonexistent for wheelchair users. The spatial map of such a building as a supermarket is very similar to a person without crutches and with crutches because of the ability of the latter to use stairs. At the same time, for the wheelchair user this map (see Bannert's experience) is different. Even the change from mechanical to electric wheelchairs brings changes in perception. The ramp incline that was so important for the mechanical wheelchair of Bannert would not require such focusing if she had an electric device.

More recently, material tools started being merged more and more with symbolic tools. Let us take such an "old" tool as a car. For a long time, this tool was almost entirely material: engine, body, wheels, steering, and braking systems. The symbolic part was limited to the speedometer and the fuel gauge, and later a radio display. The car as a mobility tool impacted very seriously on our sense of space, time, attention, and precision. However, more recently, cars became more of a hybrid nature with symbolic tools such as global positioning system (GPS) maps, rear-view displays, automatic warning systems, and a range of electronic indicators assuming more and more important roles. Once again our cognitive functions had to change in response to the changes in these tools. Displays, for example, require a degree of symbolic literacy unknown before. Some of the symbolic tools, such as a road map on paper that were so to say external, became an integral part of the car in a form of a GPS map.

Our overview of the interactions that involve material tools allows us to reach two conclusions. First, though material tools are invented for helping us to explore, control, and use our physical environment, they have a "hidden" psychological agenda. Changes in material tools lead to new demands for human psychology. Second, the more recently developed tools are less and less purely material, becoming a hybrid of material and symbolic elements. To understand this process better, we turn now to the phenomenon of symbolic tools.

Symbolic Tools as Mediators

To understand the difference between material and symbolic tools it might be instructive to look at Sébastien Leclerc's seventeenth-century print *Louis XIV Visiting the Royal Academy of Sciences* (see Figure 1.2). The purpose

Figure 1.2   Symbolic tools in Sébastien Leclerc's seventeenth-century print *Louis XIV*
Visiting the Royal Academy of Sciences
Histoire de Paris, Paris Musées/Musée Carnavalet, G.5220, CC0 (59.8 cm × 45.3 cm), 1671

of this print was to demonstrate the royal patronage of the Paris Academy of Sciences, which was established in 1666 by Louis XIV's minister Jean-Baptiste Colbert. Indeed, the first thing we see in the middle of the picture is Louis XIV himself and his entourage. The rest of the picture is rather crowded but not so much by people as by objects. Objects themselves are in a sense symbolic because they signify different sciences. On the display, there is a human skeleton as well as skeletons of different animals (biology and medicine), jars and retorts (chemistry), mirrors, and mechanical devices (physics). Some of them are just physical objects (e.g., skeletons), some mechanical devices that can be treated as material tools. But what else do we see? We see maps, plans, books, globes of the Earth, and models of the solar system. These are instruments of the other kind, because maps, books, and globes, though quite material, belong to a different type of tools: They are symbolic tools. Symbolic tools do not stand by themselves; they represent. Moreover, they often represent something, such as a distant continent, that the viewer had never seen and would probably never experience in his or her life. Unlike the material tool that interacts with here-and-now present objects and processes of the external world, symbolic tools are capable of representing objects and events distant in time and space.

Symbolic tools radically change the process of transmission of knowledge. Through the medium of written text, ancient traditions can be transmitted to the new generation without the presence of an actual storyteller as typical for preliterate societies. One does not need to be personally familiar with the coastline of Cape Cod to understand the topography of New England; this can be achieved by collecting information from written texts, maps, and drawings. Symbolic tools, however, do not just represent; they also help to encode, measure, organize, and classify. By using symbolic tools we can reduce the sequence of steps or actions to a simple code: 1, 2, 3, 4 ... or A, B, C, D .... When represented symbolically, objects become "stripped" of some of their features (e.g., the taste of apples) while other features (e.g., weight) appear as numerically coded quantities, such as 5 kg or 10 lb. A measuring tape is not just a strip of fabric or steel; it is a symbolic tool that helps us to "translate" the physical space into numbers. Being entered into a table, which is yet another symbolic tool, these numbers can be compared to other numbers that represent the length or width of other objects, and they can be added, subtracted, ordered, and so on.

Symbolic tools do not represent the entire object or event; they capture those aspects that are essential for a given purpose. The model of the solar system made of wood and brass does not aspire to capture either the matter of the planets or their size; what is represented is only their relative positions and trajectories. The map of the New World does not reflect all the physical properties of its terrain (rocks, grass, or forests); what it represents are such abstract features as the relative locations of the coastline, rivers, lakes, and mountains. In the country population tables, people are reduced to the numbers associated with the population of a specific city or rural area. Symbolic tools do not just represent but also abstract and encode some essential aspects of the objects and events.

So far, we have identified two major features of symbolic tools: First, they represent something else; and second, they represent by extracting the essence of an object or phenomenon and "translating" it into a different medium – text, numbers, drawing, and so on. We should admit, however, that our use of the notion of "tool" in connection to symbolic means was somewhat premature. Educational research provides endless examples of symbolic means made available to children that fail to become appropriated as symbolic tools. For example, reading as a simple ability to decode words and sentences does not automatically become a tool of literacy. A map in and by itself is not yet the tool of orientation in space, just as a time chart is not yet a tool for the comprehension of historical processes. All these symbolic means have the potential to become symbolic tools, but for this potential to be realized they should be appropriated not as content but as tools. We can thus present the following sequence of events associated with the acquisition and use of symbolic media:

Level 1: The presence (or absence) of certain symbolic means (e.g., texts, maps, formulae) in a given society or subculture. If these means are not available, they cannot fulfill the role of symbolic mediators.

Level 2: Certain symbolic means (e.g., texts and numbers) are available, but they appear as an integral part of content material. Their instrumental function as symbolic tools is not completely clear to novice learners.

Level 3: Novice learners are systematically introduced to symbolic means and master them as external symbolic tools (e.g., mastery in using texts for the retrieval of information, use of maps for orientation in space, use of math formulae for solving quantitative problems);

Level 4: Learners successfully internalize symbolic tools and transform them into inner "psychological tools." At this stage, literacy becomes a tool of memory and verbal thinking, the use of maps and plans transform our spatial intelligence, while tables and graphs change the way we think about organizing, comparing, and classifying data.

The fourth level reveals the distinctive feature of symbolic tools. These tools not only help us to represent, analyze, and organize information about external objects and processes, but probably more importantly they change our inner psychological processes.

While discussing the role of symbolic tools for memorization Vygotsky and Luria (1930/1984, p. 143) observed:

> Here the subject does not solve the problem by way of direct mobilization of his natural capacities; he has recourse to certain external manipulations, organizing himself through the organization of objects, creating artificial stimuli which differ from others in that they have reverse action, being directed not at other people but at himself and allowing him to solve the problem of remembering with the aid of external signs.

All psychological processes, such as perception, attention, memory, problem-solving, and decision-making, become transformed under the influence of the symbolic tools available to us. Let us, however, pay closer attention to such a basic cognitive function as memory. In preliterate society, direct memorization plays an extremely important role. The ability to recall a certain episode from the history of one's family or tribe directly depends on the person's ability to store episodes in his or her memory and then retrieve them upon request. History appears as a chain of episodes transmitted orally from generation to generation. In a literate society the same task of recalling a certain historical episode is performed using very different means and, as a result, requires different cognitive functions. In literate society words or names associated with a given historical episode become keywords used for searching various written or pictorial sources. Unlike direct memorization of an oral story told by an authoritative storyteller, a literate person activates the whole range of cognitive functions, which include the use of keywords, retrieval of information stored in various written, graphic, or pictorial texts, comparison of this information, and drawing conclusions. Thus, instead of dependence on a single cognitive function of direct memorization, people in literate societies develop and activate several cognitive functions associated with literacy, coding and decoding, systematic search, and comparison.

Moreover, though the goal of recalling a certain historical episode might be the same in oral and in literate cultures, the result is very different. In oral society information about some historical episode comes exclusively in the form of a story told by the last in a chain of storytellers. In a literate society, we have the whole collection of sources written or depicted at the time of the actual event. In the case of direct memorization, the main problem is the encoding and retrieval of information. The information is depleted in the chain of storytellers and its recall is further limited by the memorization capacity of a given person. The memory mediated by symbolic tools depends on other functions, such as an efficient search for written or pictorial sources, and their decoding, comparing, and drawing conclusions. An efficient recall of an oral story depended on the accurate reproduction of what was narrated by a storyteller; the veracity of the storyteller's account was not in question. The retrieval of written and pictorial information brings to the forefront the problem of having several, sometimes conflicting, accounts of the same episode.

Some researchers (see Olson, 1994) point to very far-reaching consequences of the change from human reliance on oral memory to reliance on literacy-based sources. One may say that in the oral tradition, the content of the historical episode and the intention of the storyteller are fused; to reproduce the story means to reproduce both the content and the intention, and this is often conveyed by such paralinguistic means as intonation, gestures, and pauses. In the literate tradition the written text, for example, a legal document, stands as a standardized form of what in oral tradition may appear as a multitude of stories:

> The use of writs and written evidence are early examples of treating written records as adequate representations of meanings – they are not employed simply as reminders of the personal beliefs and desires of the authors; their formulaic form allowed control both of the literal meaning and the speech act involved, both of which reduced openness to variable interpretations. If the complainant's original intention was lost sight of in interpreting the meaning of the document, so much the worse for that original intention. The document stands supreme. (Olson, 1994, p. 188)

The role of symbolic tools as mediators is interesting and important not only from a historical perspective, such as a transition from preliterate to literate cultures, but also for understanding the cognitive processes involved in learning and problem-solving in contemporary societies. Cognition and learning are often presented as products of individual development and the person's direct interaction with the environment (e.g., Lachman et al., 2015). Of course, no one denies the importance of such skills as reading or using numbers, but these skills appear to a certain extent as an "addition" to the main cognitive functions of perception, attention, memory, and problem-solving. The concept of symbolic mediation presented in this chapter offers a different perspective on the relationships between symbolic tools and cognition. In a sense the use of the same terms – "perception," "attention," "memory," or "problem-solving" – for direct cognitive processes and the processes mediated by symbolic tools is rather misleading. We saw this in the earlier example of the recall of a historical episode as performed via direct memorization and retrieval versus recall with the help of symbolic tools. It would be rather misleading to use the same term "memory" or "recall" for such different processes. Modern brain-imaging research has demonstrated that the processing of even a simple visual image is carried out in different brain areas by literate and illiterate people (Dehaene et al., 2010). So the use of the same term "perception" ("memory," "attention," etc.) for mental functions that may have very different mediational histories might be inappropriate. Ideally, each time we wish to talk about cognitive processes mediated by symbolic tools we should say "symbolically mediated perception," "symbolically mediated memory," "symbolically mediated problem-solving," and so on.

The problem, however, is not just terminological but conceptual. The majority of cognitive tests focus only on direct processes and avoid the issue of symbolic mediation. Let us take as an example such a function as "working memory." A considerable number of studies have linked various learning disorders as well as educational underachievement to students' poor working memory (Packiam Alloway, 2018). The standard working memory tests usually include some information to be remembered and some mental operations to be, simultaneously, performed. For example, in the Tulsky et al. (2013) Toolbox Working Memory Test participants are presented with a series of pictures of animals or pieces of food. Each picture is displayed on the computer monitor for two seconds while the name of the stimulus is simultaneously read by a computerized voice; stimuli are presented one after another, without interruption. The participants are required to remember each stimulus in a series, mentally reorder them from smallest to largest, and recite the names of the stimuli in this order. Participants begin by sequencing a two-item string and with each correct response the string is increased by one item, up to a maximum of seven items. If the participants are unable to sequence the string correctly, they are provided with a second trial of the same number of items; the task is discontinued when the participant provides incorrect responses on two trials with the same number of items or when the participant correctly sequences all seven items. In other words, the working memory is tested under conditions when all operations should be performed in the head without any possibility of employing external tools.

The symbolic tools alternative in a study of memory, however, had already been proposed in the 1930s. Alexander Luria, one of the pioneers of the sociocultural approach, argued that it would be important to compare direct memorization with memorization mediated by such external symbolic tools as pictograms (Luria, 1979, p. 50). First, the participants' direct memorization of a long list of words and phrases was examined, after which they were informed that after hearing each word or phrase they can draw some pictographic symbol which later may help them to recall the word. The procedure thus allowed comparing two different types of memory: direct and symbolically mediated. Moreover, it became possible to see what kind of pictogram is effective in helping to memorize more abstract concepts, such as "hard work." Luria's "Pictograms Test" is still included in the standard battery of cognitive tests used in Russia (Rimskaja and Rimskij, 1999).

It does not require much imagination to understand that some versions of the pictogram test can also be used for the examination of working memory. It would allow us to identify children who perform poorly on "direct" working memory tests but benefit more than others from the external symbolic mediators. Moreover, such a procedure would help identify which stage of the working memory operation – retention of information or manipulation with it – is more sensitive to external symbolic mediation. And yet, to the best of our knowledge, there has been no attempt to include symbolically mediated trials in the recent working memory tests.

The lack of interest in mediated memory appears truly paradoxical if one takes into account the fact that some of the interventions proposed for children with poor working memory are based exactly on the use of such symbolic tools as graphic organizers. For example, Gillam et al. (2018) argued that instead of trying to improve the working memory capacity itself, the problem can be "bypassed" by providing children with more effective information-processing strategies. The development of these strategies, in their turn, is facilitated by the use of icons, concept maps, and graphic organizers.

The educational importance of symbolic tools is not limited to the area of working memory. The importance of distinguishing between direct and symbolically mediated problem-solving can be illustrated by the following study conducted by van Garderen and Montague (2003). The researchers first investigated the spontaneous use of diagrams for solving math problems among children who experienced serious math difficulties, average students, and students with high achievement in math. The study revealed that children with math difficulties used symbolic representations significantly less frequently than other students. One may claim that these children used only direct math problem-solving, while other children used both direct and symbolically mediated problem-solving. Moreover, when low-performance children did use representations their representations were of a pictorial rather than diagrammatic nature. One can easily understand that a depiction of a child on a bike does not help much in solving the math problem about the time needed for a journey from point A to point B and then to point C. Children with high achievement in math spontaneously created diagrammatic representations of a problem (e.g., a line connecting points A, B, and C with the time spent for each leg of the travel inserted into the diagram) more often than other children. So, what we can see here are three different types of problem-solving: problem-solving mediated by the relevant diagrammatic symbolic tool, problem-solving accompanied by an irrelevant pictorial image, and direct problem-solving unaccompanied by any symbolic mediation. In a sense, these are three very different processes that use different cognitive functions, the processes that should not be covered by the same term "math problem-solving." The lack of problem-solving mediated by diagrams is, however, not a "destiny"; van Garderen and her colleagues successfully taught children with learning disorders how to use diagrams for problem-solving and thus improved their math performance.

Some additional instances of mediation via symbolic tools are discussed in greater detail in Chapter 2. For now, we summarize some of the main points of the symbolic tools paradigm. First, symbolic tools represent objects, processes, and relationships in a form created by a given culture and inherent to a given culture (texts, numbers, charts, etc.). Second, a symbolic form is not "intuitive" in the sense that the acquisition of symbolic languages requires systematic learning. Though this fact is often overlooked, much of formal education consists of students' acquisition and internalization of symbolic tools. Third, the use of symbolic tools in learning and problem-solving leads to the development in the human mind of a parallel "line" of cognitive functions, such as symbolically mediated perception, attention, memory, and so on.

Human Mediators

The third class of mediators is people. Mothers by and large serve as reliable mediators between young children and their environment. Mothers select objects and events to which children are exposed, sometimes emphasize or on the contrary downplay certain aspects of the exposure, interpret environmental events to children, prevent children from entering into dangerous situations, etc. Of course, parents are not the only human mediators; teachers and other mentors take over some of the mediator's functions while guiding children through the cultural environment of formal and informal learning.

Examination of the role of human mediators helps us to understand better such phenomena as learning deprivation, developmental difficulties, and alienation.

One of the possible starting points for the discussion about human mediation is the well-known study of Rene Spitz (1945) in which he linked the phenomenon of so-called hospitalism to early maternal deprivation. Spitz followed two groups of children. The first group was raised in an orphanage, where the babies were well provided for in terms of their physical needs but were severely deprived of contact with a permanent mother figure. The second group of babies was raised in a nursery in a prison where their mothers were incarcerated. The mothers were allowed to give their babies care and affection every day. The motor and cognitive development of children brought us in the orphanage lagged significantly behind those reared in the prison nursery. The orphanage children were also less curious and less playful. At an older age, many of the orphanage children ended up in institutions for children with intellectual disabilities and mental health problems. Spitz thus pointed out that the relative physical comfort and sufficient nutrition provided in the orphanages are not sufficient for supporting the normative development of the child – the presence of the permanent human mediation, a mother figure, is a crucial factor for such development.

A similar line of reasoning about the importance of human mediators during early childhood was developed somewhat later by John Bowlby and Mary Ainsworth (see Ainsworth, 1962) and became known as attachment theory. The gist of this theory is that a strong emotional and physical attachment to a primary caregiver (mother figure) is critical for a child's normative development. Bowlby and Ainsworth pointed out that there are different situations in which proper maternal mediation fails to take place. The first situation is institutional when the child is brought up in an institution rather than a family and does not have permanent contact with a mother figure; the second situation is associated with insufficient or distorted interaction between the mother (or mother figure) and the child at home; the third situation is associated with the child's inability to interact with a mother figure even though she is present and ready to provide sufficient contact and care. Such an inability to interact might be caused by repeated breaches of ties with mother figures or some previous deprivation experiences.

Ainsworth (1962) identified several crucial questions related to maternal deprivation. The first question is about the age at which maternal deprivation took place. Are there periods that are particularly sensitive to maternal deprivation? In other words, at what age does deprivation have the most damaging impact on a child's development? The second question is about the amount of developmental damage caused by maternal deprivation and the specificity of this damage, for example, intellectual, emotional, or behavioral. The third question is the question of the permanence of the damage and the child's resilience. To what extent can the damage caused by earlier maternal deprivation be somewhat compensated at a later age? All these questions continue to challenge researchers who, however, do not necessarily view them from the perspective of Bowlby's attachment theory. This leads us to the next "station" in the history of human mediation research: the mediated learning experience theory of Reuven Feuerstein (see Feuerstein and Rand, 1974).

The initial psychological and educational observations were made by Feuerstein during his work with various groups of "deprived" children: children survivors of the Holocaust and refugee and immigrant children from North Africa. By the standards of attachment theory, some of these children failed to establish a secure attachment to their mother figure because they were often separated from their families. Feuerstein, however, reached beyond the problem of the attachment to a mother figure and pointed out a more general phenomenon of "cultural deprivation." The situation of cultural deprivation occurs when for some reason, to be discussed later, the transmission of culture from parents or other primary caregivers to a child is disrupted. Feuerstein identified several possible causes of such disruption, some of them associated with radical changes in the children's environment, others with particular features of the children themselves or/and their parents (see Feuerstein et al., 1980, chapter 3). For example, the relocation of the family from a traditional small rural community to the outskirts of a large city may result in the breakdown of the extended family, abandonment of the traditional cultural roles by its members, and as a result disruption in the cultural transmission from generation to generation. Children become alienated from their family's culture. This is how Feuerstein described the consequences of the relocation of Jewish Moroccan families from isolated rural communities to the city slums:

> With the move to the city slums, with its crowded conditions of life, migration of the entire extended family was not possible, and life became organized around the restricted nuclear family. Within this new family framework, with its absence of vertical and lateral components, the amount of mediated learning experience was considerably reduced. Responsibility for the transfer of cultural transmission shifted from the family circle to

the institutions like the Heder and Kutab (Jewish and Muslim religious schools), without these institutions being equipped to meet even the most rudimentary scholastic skills required by the child, let alone the transmission of his substantial cultural heritage. In many cases, the outcome for the child was a void; he was deprived of a meaningful cultural identity to which he could relate. (Feuerstein et al., 1980, p. 40)

Of course, it is not only a radical change in the environment that disrupts cultural transmission. In the period when Feuerstein collected his data (i.e., the 1950s to 1970s), it was acceptable to consider a child born with some genetic disorder (e.g., Down syndrome) as permanently mentally retarded. When parents received such a diagnosis from the child's pediatrician their natural reaction was to abandon the very idea of trying to transmit their culture to the retarded child. The child remained culturally deprived because his/her parents concluded that the transmission of culture is futile due to the child's special needs. A different version of the cultural deprivation of children with special needs (e.g., Down syndrome) takes place when parents are quite eager to mediate their culture to the child, but do not know how to do this. All their previous experience has been with typically developing children and no one instructed them how and what to mediate to a child with Down syndrome. Finally, it is not only the special needs of children that may deter parents from actively engaging in the transmission of culture – this can simply be the child's gender. In some communities, the type of culture considered suitable for boys and girls is very different. In many cases, the range of cultural skills transmitted to boys is much broader than those intended for girls. The girls, thus, become intentionally culturally deprived simply because of their gender.

All these examples belong to what can be defined as a societal level of human mediation: mediation aimed at the transmission of culture from generation to generation. When using the term "culture" it is important to remember that Feuerstein was primarily concerned with the transmission process itself rather than the content of the transmitted culture (Feuerstein and Hoffman, 1982). In his opinion, cultural deprivation is damaging to the child's development first of all because the child becomes deprived of the cognitive and learning skills that otherwise are developed in the process of cultural transmission. While on the societal level, human mediation appears as a transmission of culture, on the individual level it manifests itself as a quality of interaction between a child, a task the child is facing, and an adult who provides mediation to a child.

This is how Feuerstein defined this type of interaction:

> The mediated learning experience can be defined as a quality of interaction between child and environment which depends on the activity of an initiated and intentioned adult who interposes him/herself between the child and the world. In the process of such mediation, the adult selects and frames stimuli for the child creates artificial schedules and sequences of stimuli, removes certain stimuli and makes the other stimuli more conspicuous … Mediated learning experiences are a very important condition for the development of the very unique human conditions of modifiability, or the capacity to benefit from exposure to stimuli in a more generalized way than is usually the case. (Feuerstein, 1991, p. 26)

Feuerstein went considerably further than other psychologists in emphasizing the paramount importance of human mediation for the development of the child. First of all, he proposed dividing all learning processes into two large classes: direct learning and human-mediated learning. Second, he suggested that not all situations that involve a child, a task, and an adult qualify as leading to the mediated learning experience (MLE). He elaborated on specific criteria of MLE that help to distinguish between interactions that have the MLE quality and those that do not. Finally, and probably most ambitious, Feuerstein claimed that a rich MLE leads to greater cognitive modifiability of the child and paves the way to more efficient direct learning. An insufficient amount of MLE in his opinion is one of the main causes of learning difficulties and even cognitive disabilities (see Feuerstein and Rand, 1974; Feuerstein et al., 1980).

To understand better how human mediation may impact early child development, let us consider the following study by Pnina Klein (2000) on babies with very low birth weight. Very low birth weight is known to be a high-risk factor in terms of the child's development. Klein examined the quality of mother–child mediation and cognitive development of infants with a birth weight below 1.5 kg. The quality of mediation was identified by using the observation scale that focused on five MLE criteria formulated by Feuerstein and further elaborated by Klein.

The first criterion is intentionality or focusing. The adult makes a deliberate effort to draw a child's attention to a certain object or task by establishing eye contact with a child, moving objects, placing toys within a child's reach, scheduling stimuli, and so on. Intentionality or focusing achieves its goal when reciprocated by the child who responds vocally or gesturally.

The second criterion is the mediation of meaning or "exiting." The goal of this mediation is to emphasize the emotional and energetic value of a child's and adult's actions – "this is why we do this!" Emotional emphasis can be achieved by vocal emphasis, gestures, or words themselves.

The third criterion is transcendence or expanding. According to Feuerstein and Klein, even young children should learn how to look beyond the "here and now" situation. The current episode should be connected to the past and future, the current location to other locations, and objects should be explored beyond their current practical role (e.g., water during bathing is not just for bathing).

The fourth criterion is the mediation of feelings of competence or encouragement. The young child should not only become competent in performing some actions but also become aware of his/her competence. Often the affirmation of the child's success – "good," "excellent," and "well done" – is accompanied by an explanation given to a child why his/her action was successful.

The fifth criterion is the regulation of behavior. The mediating adult helps the child to regulate his/her behavior by facilitating the beginning of the action, for example, "First, turn all the pieces over, then search for the right piece," or on the contrary by preventing the impulsive action, for example, "It is hot; cool it first before putting in the mouth" (Klein, 2000, p. 242).

The study conducted by Klein demonstrated that the quality of parent–child mediation strongly correlated with the cognitive performance of the children, while no significant correlation was found between the child's birth weight and the same cognitive measures. In other words, the quality of human mediation proved to be a better predictor of the children's cognitive development than their birth weight.

If parent–child mediation proved to be able to overcome some of the developmental problems usually associated with low birth weight, what about such social factors as the low socioeconomic status (SES) of the child's family? That was a question posed in another study conducted by Klein and her colleagues (Klein et al., 1987). The study involved typically developing children from low-SES families and their mothers. The families were considered to belong to a "high-risk" group because of their status: about 60 percent of the sample were single mothers, some of them had not finished high school, and on average the entire sample demonstrated rather low performance in a standard language test. The study was longitudinal, lasting four years. Mother–child interactions were observed during the free-play sessions at four, eight, twelve, twenty-four, and thirty-six months using the MLE observation scale described earlier. Infants' level of development was evaluated periodically using Bayley Scales between four and twenty-four months and McCarthy Scales between thirty-six and forty-eight months.

The study produced several interesting findings, the most significant among them is a strong correlation between the quality of MLE interaction at the age of twelve months and the child's cognitive performance at the age of four. In other words, though all children belonged to "high-risk" families, those children who received more quality MLE starting at an early age had a better chance of more successful development. A somewhat less optimistic finding was the relative stability of the MLE profile of the mother. Mothers who started as stronger mediators continued to be stronger, while weaker mediators remained weaker; this is even though the average level of mediation of all mothers grew over time.

One of the distinctive features of Feuerstein's theory of MLE was his belief in the reversibility of cognitive impairment caused by insufficient mediation at an earlier age. Though Feuerstein agreed that there might be optimal periods for specific forms of mediation, he was very much against the idea of so-called critical periods. The concept of critical periods stipulates that there are specific developmental "windows of opportunity" for certain psychological functions. If the function failed to be developed until a certain age, the damage is permanent. Feuerstein, on the contrary, claimed that intensive human mediation even at an older age can significantly improve underdeveloped cognitive functions. To prove his point Feuerstein offered a number of clinical case studies all of them having a somewhat similar "storyline": The lack of quality MLE at an early age (for a wide variety of reasons) leading to cognitive and behavioral difficulties, identification of the child's problems at an older age, intensive MLE-based treatment of the child and family therapy ultimately leading to the much higher achievement of the child than ever expected.

Here is a description of one such case. Feuerstein and his team were asked to examine 6-year-old K with the purpose of deciding whether he should remain for another year in kindergarten or be placed in the first grade of the school for educable mentally retarded children. At the time of examination, the standard intelligence score (IQ) of K was in the seventies, corresponding to that of an educable mentally retarded child. In addition to cognitive problems, K was reported to have poor attention, restlessness, and a lack of cooperation with adults. The examination of K revealed two rather unexpected features, the first being K's excellent cooperation with assessors, his willingness and ability to work with different tasks for several hours, and in general much better learning than one would predict on the basis of his poor IQ scores. The second feature was the rather surprising reaction of K's mother who continued to insist that her son was retarded and that his retardation had an organic nature. She rejected Feuerstein's recommendation to place K in a regular first grade simultaneously with giving him an intensive cognitive treatment program. K's mother seemed to be very detached from her child, though she claimed that his birth was not "an accident," that she wanted him, and that his early development was normal. It was only later when Feuerstein demonstrated to the mother even greater progress made by K that the real story came to the surface. Contrary to the mother's original "story," K was not her biological son – he was adopted from an ethnic group other than her own. The mother had a strong prejudice against this group and was convinced that its members cannot reach a high intellectual level. She deliberately and systematically distanced herself from K, so that the child grew up with a very limited MLE. The breakthrough in K's development came from the concerted intervention with K himself and his adopted family. K received MLE-based cognitive training, his father, who proved to be a better mediator, assumed a more active role in K's rearing, and even the mother accepted the fact that K had a much higher learning ability than she previously thought. The lack of MLE at K's earlier age became compensated by the intensive infusion of MLE at his school age (see Feuerstein et al., 2006, p. 110).

Feuerstein's concept of MLE and the claim of its centrality in child development has several important practical implications for both the assessment and the educational practice. In what concerns the assessment, Feuerstein proposed the MLE-based interactive assessment as an alternative to standard cognitive testing (Feuerstein et al., 1979). During standard cognitive testing, the examinee is directly confronted by the assessment tasks; the assessor's role is just to provide the tasks and record the examinee's responses. According to Feuerstein such an unmediated assessment is capable of identifying only the already well-established cognitive skills but is powerless to uncover the examinee's LP. The "secret" of LP assessment, according to Feuerstein, lies in the active infusion of MLE into the assessment procedure. The assessor in Feuerstein's model ceases to be a passive provider of test items and becomes an active mediator. The assessment becomes interactive with the assessor actively drawing the examinees' attention (MLE criterion of intentionality), explaining the reason for each task (mediation of meaning), and helping the examinee to identify the general principle behind the whole group of progressively more challenging tasks (mediation of transcendence). In this alternative model, the border between assessment and intervention is crossed; assessment ceases to be an examination of pre-existing abilities and becomes an examination of cognitive and behavioral changes that take place during the assessment itself.

Similarities and differences between Feuerstein's and other concepts of LP are discussed in Chapter 4; at the moment, it is important to emphasize that for Feuerstein only the assessment infused with MLE qualified as a viable alternative to typical, direct cognitive tests.

Assessment, however, is not the only area that appears in a different light when one takes into account the phenomenon of MLE. Learning in general and classroom learning in particular also appear from a different perspective. The situation of direct learning includes direct, unmediated interaction between learning material and the child's mind. The learning material may take the form of a book, a film, a lecture, or an environment independently explored by the child. What is not included in direct learning is a human mediator who "stands" between the learning material and the learner and mediates this material to the child according to the criteria of MLE. Direct learning is the predominant form of learning in adults and those children who successfully developed the skills of self-directed learning. However, younger children and many older children and adults don't have sufficient direct learning skills, and as a result don't benefit much from the situations of direct learning. Some of them become defined as underachievers or learning disabled. When the child does not know how to accept the material, cannot identify its meaning, or does not know how to respond, the second type of learning, the mediated one, becomes crucially important.

Of course, many teachers infuse their teaching with MLE without ever hearing about Feuerstein or his theory. We may call them "spontaneous mediators." However, as testified by the continuing public frustration with the educational process, these "spontaneous mediators" constitute the pedagogical exception rather than the rule.

What then is the classroom pedagogy of teachers-mediators? To start with, let us define what teachers-mediators do not do. They do not deliver a pre-prepared lecture only because "it is important to cover the material." On the other hand, they also do not let children "explore things themselves" without any plan or guidance from the teacher. What distinguishes teachers-mediators is their greater awareness of "how," while the majority of teachers focus mainly on "what." With greater availability of learning materials online, the teacher's role is no longer that of a supplier of otherwise unavailable information (as it was in the past); their role is to be a mediator who helps students to process and understand information. So, the focal point is not the "what" kind of information to transmit but the "how" to process this information. As a result of this emphasis, teachers-mediators are expected to be capable of understanding not only the scope of students' content knowledge but also their cognitive needs. A considerable amount of difficulties experienced by students do not stem from the lack of specific knowledge or operations but from the more general learning deficiencies originating in the underdevelopment of such cognitive processes as orientation, comparison, planning, and drawing conclusions. One of the primary goals of teachers-mediators is to check to what extent students' difficulties are associated with the lack of mastery of specific operations (e.g., multiplication or division) and to what extent these difficulties might be related to much more general problems such as separating relevant and irrelevant data in the given math task. Once the students' cognitive needs are identified, teachers-mediators start infusing their curricular lessons with the necessary cognitive exercises.

The entire pedagogical process promoted by teachers-mediators is shaped by the criteria of MLE. They plan how to keep students' attention and how to convey to the students the feeling of the teacher's strong interest in the students' learning (*mediation of intentionality* or *focusing*). The other side of *intentionality* is *reciprocity*: the teacher's sensitivity to students' responses and readiness to change the flow of the lesson in order to respond to the students emerging learning needs. In general, flexibility is one of the primary distinctive features of the teachers-mediators. Once the students' attention is captured, teachers-mediators start mediating the learning tasks to them. These tasks, however, are never presented as just here-and-now concrete exercises, they always contain the potential for generalization and transfer (*mediation of transcendence* or *expanding*). The simplest task, such as "Johnny has five toy cars, and his brother Benny has three cars more, how many toy cars do they have together?" can be turned into the starting point for a deeper analysis of, for example, relevant vs. irrelevant data. Is it relevant that Johnny is called Johnny and Benny is called Benny? Is it relevant that they are brothers? What is the meaning of the phrase "three cars more"? In other words, teachers-mediators guide their students to extract the math meaning from the text that appears as a description of an everyday situation. Obviously, such an activity is much more general and expandable than just teaching a simple operation $5 + 5 + 3 = 13$. The mediational emphasis on transcendence responds to one of the primary requirements of contemporary education: teaching students how to handle problems other than those they solved in the classroom.

All criteria of MLE are interconnected, and *transcendence* is closely connected to the other criterion: *mediation of meaning*. In the earlier example with toy cars, we mentioned that instead of teaching just a concrete operation of addition, teachers-mediators help children to extract mathematical meaning from the task that appears as a simple everyday situation. To the implicit or explicit children's question "why do we do this?" teachers-mediators explain that one of the ways to understand the world around us is through its quantitative and spatial relations. In this "picture" of the world it is not important that Johnny is called Johnny and Benny is called Benny or that they are brothers; what is important is the quantitative aspect. The teacher-mediator does not stop here but expands further by showing that the same episode with toy cars can be understood not only in a quantitative way. For example, if we wish to see the linguistic rather than the mathematical meaning of the same episode, the quantities themselves become not very important while their verbal form comes to the forefront, thus Benny has "three *cars* more," but if he had "one *car* more," it would be different not only quantitatively but also linguistically: the plural form marked by "s" as opposed to an unmarked singular. *Mediation of meaning* helps children to understand that classroom exercises are not about products they generate, such as solved math tasks or written exercises, but about processes they involve. These processes provide students with the ability to comprehend the world in a number of ways: mathematically, linguistically, historically, biologically, etc.

Are Feuerstein's criteria of MLE the only way to describe human mediation? Of course not! The criteria of MLE formulated by Feuerstein offer only one model of adult–child mediation. Another way of characterizing the adults' mediation with children is via a concept of scaffolding (Marmelshtine, 2017; Wood et al., 1976). As suggested by the very word scaffolding, the meditation provided by adults to children reminds us of creating a scaffold that helps children who "stand" on it to master a new task. Wood and his colleagues tested how a dyad of child–adult will construct a three-dimensional wooden structure. The design of the task was such that it was likely to be beyond children's current skills but could be achieved with the help of an adult mediator. Mothers proved to be quite skillful mediators to their 4- to 5-year-old children – most of the time they did not intervene in operations that children were able to perform themselves but provided support with problems situated one level above those mastered by the child. The same interaction interpreted from the child's side suggests that children have a certain "region of sensitivity" to the adult's help, the "region" just above the current performance level of the child themselves.

The process of scaffolding ideally should include recruitment of interest, task simplification, direction maintenance, identifying critical features, frustration control, demonstration, and transfer of responsibility. One can see here both cognitive and emotional scaffolds. Task simplification, identifying critical features of the task, and demonstrating the necessary operations are more cognitive, while frustration control and the generally positive attitude of adults provide an emotional scaffold. The transfer of responsibility is very important; without it, scaffolding would not fulfill its goal which is supporting the child's mastery of more challenging tasks.

The quality of scaffolding and ultimately its contribution to child development depends on the adults' ability to attune their assistance to the child's dynamically changing performance. Successful scaffolding is always provided in the "region of sensitivity" in which children both need assistance and are capable of receiving assistance. The more successful scaffolding has been shown to relate to better cognitive performance in preschool and school age, greater classroom competence, arithmetic skills, early reading, and reading comprehension (see Marmelshtine, 2017).

Though the scaffolding research focused on child–adult joint activity, it is not difficult to see that many of the parameters of scaffolding apply to any novice–mentor situation. The central element of scaffolding – the mentor's ability to contingently respond to the novice's performance – is also the central element of any successful training activity. Let us project the scaffolding parameters into the field of higher education. The job of a professor is to recruit students' interest, map the critical features of the subject area, adjust the material to the level just above the students' level of current knowledge, help students maintain focus on the selected topic (direction maintenance), provide frustration control caused by poor exam results or time pressure, demonstrate model solutions of the problems and tasks, and ultimately prepare students to become experts and mentors (transfer of responsibility).

Mediation via Activities

The last form of mediation to be discussed in this chapter is mediation via activities. We have already touched on the issue of activities when we discussed the mediational role of tools, both physical and symbolic. An introduction of a new symbolic tool (e.g., writing) creates possibilities for new activities, such as literacy-based education. It seems, however, that one should distinguish between the impact of tools themselves and the impact of various activities that incorporate these tools. The symbolic tool of writing can be used not only in different educational activities but also in work activities, religious activities, and so on. The same symbolic tool promotes various activities but also becomes part of various activities. Human mediation (e.g., intentionality or focusing) can also be incorporated into various activities within which mediation of focusing takes place. In other words, our behavior and cognition are shaped not only by the tools we use or human mediation we display but also by the activities we are engaged in.

The impact of the dominant types of human activities on human life and civilization has, for a long time, occupied both historians and anthropologists. One of the still hotly debated questions, for example, is the possible changes caused in prehistoric times by the transition from the hunter-gatherer lifestyle to sedentary agriculture (Cummings et al., 2018). The subsistence of hunters and gatherers was based on such activities as hunting wild animals, fishing, and gathering wild edible plants, without the domestication of plants or animals, probably except dogs. Many of the hunter-gatherer groups were nomadic. Now let us compare this to sedentary agriculture which includes such activities as the cultivation and storage of selected crops, domestication of animals, and the use of them in agricultural work. It is not just tools and even mainly not tools but subsistence activities themselves that distinguished settled agriculturalists from nomadic hunters and gatherers.

For the purpose of our discussion about the mediational role of activities, however, we don't need archeological data; it is sufficient to concentrate on the main types of human activities prevalent in contemporary industrial and post-industrial societies. Of course, it is impossible to compile an exhaustive list, but focusing on the following main activities is sufficient for our purpose. These activities are learning, play, work, practical (the activity of daily living), interpersonal (including parenting), spiritual, and destructive activities (e.g., terrorism).

First of all, each one of these activities is sociocultural by its very nature and therefore their mediational impacts on human behavior and cognition are socioculturally specific. Different social and cultural groups develop their own versions of these activities. Manual work is different from information-based work. Both of these types of work activities have certain similar features that distinguish them from, let us say, play activities, but at the same time, each of them has different possibilities for shaping human behavior and cognition.

Second, the mediational role of activities can be examined both developmentally and structurally. The developmental perspective is discussed in greater detail in Chapter 3; right now, it is sufficient to mention that from the sociocultural perspective child development can be conceptualized as a transition from one leading activity to another (Karpov, 2005). Of course, during each period of their development children are engaged in various activities (interpersonal, play, learning, etc.) but according to the model of leading activities, in each developmental period there is one activity that plays the leading role and is crucial for propelling the child's cognitive and emotional development. The leading activities are shaped by a given culture and subculture and they reflect both the child's level of maturation and the expectations of their parents and other mentors.

The model of leading activities is very different from the typical developmental theory that perceives children's activities as a product of child maturation. For example, the famous developmental stages described by Piaget (1950) – sensory-motor, preoperational, concrete-operational, and formal operational – are characterized by the type of cognitive abilities demonstrated by children. Once a given ability is mature enough, children are perceived as ready to become engaged in the activities that utilize these abilities.

The leading activities model, on the contrary, positions leading activities as a driving force of child development. Within each one of the developmental periods, the child's cognitive and interpersonal skills lead to the formation of a new motive that corresponds to the new leading activity of the next developmental period. For example, the interpersonal component is central during the earliest period in child development, while play in a form of sensory-motor manipulation with toys plays a subdominant role. Gradually, however, the object-centered joint play activity with adults becomes a new motive of the child and at a certain moment assumes the role of the leading activity with emotional contact becoming subdominant. Similarly, the leading activity of object-centered play gradually prepares the child for the transition to sociodramatic play. For example, if during the first of these two periods, manipulation with a toy car is central, in the second period the imaginary role of a driver becomes the main interest of the child, with a toy car relegated to the subdominant role of one of the play's physical prompts.

As is already clear from these examples, one should distinguish between an activity (e.g., play when it becomes a leading activity) and "the same" activity when it has a subdominant role. This distinction leads us to the second perspective on activities as mediators: the structural one. While the developmental perspective shows how the transition from one leading activity to the next one promotes child development, the structural perspective provides a simultaneous view of the activities we are involved in.

Let us consider activities in which a modern female person (P) is engaged during what can be described as a typical day. The day usually starts with many practical activities, such as washing, dressing, and preparing and eating breakfast. The everyday nature and practicality of these activities shape P's perception of hygiene, nutrition, clothing, etc. She thinks about them with the help of everyday concepts: pleasant, tasty, fashionable, and so on. As we will see later, once "the same" objects such as food, detergents, and fabrics become targets of the work activity, their perception and understanding take place in very different, work-oriented or scientific concepts.

Returning to P's morning, let us assume that she is married and a mother of two children. The practical activities of the morning become intertwined with various interpersonal activities. Already at this stage, one may ask a question about the possible hierarchy of the activities, namely, is the interpersonal activity ("making husband and children happy") dominant for P, while practical aspects are secondary, or on the contrary is practical activity ("efficient preparation for leaving home") dominant for her? Skipping the possible additional practical activities, let us follow P to her place of work.

Though the work may appear as a pretty straightforward type of activity, such an assumption can be misleading. While it is often taken for granted that in the workplace, the work is done and in return salaries are paid, the activities in which participants are engaged might be other than work. Just imagine that the male boss of P perceives the workplace primarily as an arena for bolstering his personal image. The work for him, thus, is just a context for the dominant interpersonal type of activity. This sets the scene for the possible conflict of activity involvement. P views all things including relationships between co-workers through the prism of the work activity as a dominant one; her boss, on the other hand, perceived the same relationships as interpersonal. The workplace thinking of P is shaped by the considerations related to the work process and its products (planning, execution, technologies, etc.). The workplace thinking of her boss is shaped by possible interpersonal alliances. Quite often the so-called differences of opinion that emerge during the job meetings do not stem from the different analyses of the same process or product but from the profoundly different implicit activities in which members of the work team are involved.

As mentioned in the "morning" episode, "the same" objects (e.g., detergents, foods, or fabrics) are conceptualized very differently in the context of work activity in contrast to practical activity. A pleasantly smelling soap or shampoo in the morning becomes an object determined by its chemical and physical properties in the context of industrial production or laboratory testing processes. The switch of dominant activity from practical to job related or learning related sometimes leads to surprising results. As was shown in the often-quoted study of Lave (1988), "the same" operation of proportional reasoning turned out to be very different when presented as a practical task of supermarket shopping and as an abstractive math task. In Lave's opinion, the difference was related to the difference in activities; it was not an abstract math operation transferred from the field of formal learning to everyday shopping. The participants in Lave's experiments preserved "the same" problems differently because these problems were mediated by different activities.

P's workday is over and after briefly checking on her children (practical and interpersonal activities) she heads to the drama studio in which she is a permanent member. Of course, as in any association, the relationships between studio members can be shaped in part by interpersonal activities. For our purpose, however, we focus on other activities that shape P's behavior and thinking in the context of the drama studio. This allows us to see how different activities potentially coexist in the same context. The first activity that we see in the drama studio is learning. The head of the studio teaches the member how to perform and how to become amateur actors. Because the studio is not a commercial theater its activity is in some respects similar to the school. As in school, the real product is a student who becomes a self-directed learner, while the task, exams, and essays are just a means of learning rather than its products. In the same way in this studio, the final performance to be staged by its members is just the means for becoming amateur actors. However, learning is not the only activity P is involved in at the studio. The most interesting activity is play, and play here appears in two different forms. P imagines herself as an actress in very much the same way as a child may imagine himself to be a truck driver or a policeman. While in the studio, she plays the imaginary role of an actress. In addition, however, there is her role in the play the studio is rehearsing and staging. If the play in question is *Hamlet*, P may be involved in the play activity of being Ophelia or Gertrude. It is not difficult to understand that there are considerable differences between just reading *Hamlet* as a part of a learning activity and playing one of the characters, in a sense of looking at the text of the tragedy "from within."

We followed P through her activities during the typical day to emphasize that it is not only physical and symbolic tools, and not only human mediation, that mediates our perception and understanding of objects, processes, and events. Various activities developed in human society such as work, play, and practical and interpersonal activities each influence our behavior and cognition. These activities are among the central elements of the theory of the cultural mind. Even when alone, a person is always involved in the activities constructed and made available by a given culture and society.

We started this chapter by posing the question about the character of people's interactions with their environments. Are these interactions direct and natural, or mediated and cultural? We then proceeded to show that if we wish to understand the human cultural mind we should focus on those mediators that stand "between" people and their environments. It turned out that there are different types of mediators and that they function in a variety of ways. Some of them, such as physical tools, are primarily aimed at producing changes in the environment, but the change of physical tools may prompt the development of new cognitive abilities or at least activation of the pre-existing but rarely used ones. Symbolic tools, on the other hand, are directly related to changes in the "cultural mind" by moving it farther from immediate interaction with the environment to interactions based on symbolic representations (texts, maps, graphs, formulae, etc.). For physical and symbolic tools to become mediators, they should be mediated to novices by experts. So, human mediation and its specific parameters turn out to be essential for child development, education, and the acquisition of culture. Throughout human history, human mediation in combination with symbolic and physical tools becomes "packaged" into various activities, such as work, play, and practical activities. These activities thus become another class of mediators that interpose themselves between the cultural mind and the environment. The mediational perspective thus offers us new conceptual tools for inquiring about child development, learning, education, and thinking.

CHAPTER 2

Symbolic Tools and Mental Functions

As mentioned in Chapter 1, it is impossible to imagine a culture that does not have symbolic mediators. One may even say that the world of culture actually starts with the invention and the use of signs and symbols. Spoken language and pictorial images are probably the most ancient symbolic mediators. But what is a symbol? Dictionaries usually define a symbol as a mark or character used as a conventional representation of an object, function, or process. Thus, $ represents the dollar currency; F $(x) = 2\,x^2$ represents the relationship between the argument and the function, symbol x in its turn represents the argument, while symbol F represents the function; as a traffic sign ⌐→ represents the direction in which the traffic must turn. Two important concepts are present in these definitions of symbol: "representation" and "convention." At the same time, we think that another concept is missing in this definition: the concept of "tool." Of course, verbal or pictorial symbols represent objects and processes, and of course, they become symbols only because there is an agreed-upon convention that links symbols to the object or process that they symbolize. The sounds Y-E-S symbolize agreement or affirmation because such is the convention of the users of the English language. For those familiar with one of the particular symbolic conventions, the sign © symbolizes copyright; it is important to remember, however, that for those unfamiliar with this convention this is just a semi-circle embedded into a larger circle. Later we return to the important question about the representational role of symbols and about the ways in which conventions linking them to objects, concepts, and processes are transmitted from generation to generation. Right now, however, it is important to focus on what is missing in the typical definition of symbols, namely their potential role as tools.

The moment we use the word "tool," we become confronted with the issue of similarity and difference between material and symbolic tools. The very notion of tool usually evokes in our mind an image of a material tool such as a knife or a brush. As mentioned in Chapter 1, what is common to all material tools is their action directed toward changes in the physical world: the world of objects. A knife helps us to change the shape of a piece of wood so that it becomes a walking stick or a fishing rod. A brush changes the appearance of objects because it "mediates" between the paint and the object to be painted. The main function of material tools is to change objects or processes in the outside world. The structure and properties of the tool (e.g., its shape, weight, or sharpness) predetermine its instrumental role.

The instrumental properties of symbolic tools are very different. They do not aim at changing objects; instead, they represent, organize, and transform information about objects and events. In the course of this representation and transformation they also change our thinking processes. This is the main difference between material and symbolic tools; while material tools are directed "outwards" – from a person toward the world of objects – symbolic tools are directed "inwards" toward the thinking processes of people themselves. Thus, two parallel histories of tools can be written: a history of material tools, from a stone axe to modern mechanical tools; and a history of symbolic tools, from primitive signs and drawings to texts, maps, formulae, and diagrams. Some researchers (Luria, 1976) even claim that pivotal moments in human history can be understood as a radical transition from thinking based on immediate experiences to knowledge and understanding based on the use of symbolic tools.

A Quasi-historical Experiment

This claim was put to the test by Vygotsky and Luria through a "quasi-historical" field study conducted in Soviet Central Asia in the early 1930s. The logic of such a study was as follows. Since it is impossible to conduct an empirical study of historical changes occurring in human cognition, the best approximation would be to study a traditional society with technology, lifestyle, and learning patterns more or less corresponding to the previous historical periods that undergoes a rapid sociocultural change. Vygotsky and Luria thought that they had found such a natural historical "experiment" in Soviet Central Asia during the early 1930s. The unique sociocultural situation of this region in the late 1920s and early 1930s was determined by a very rapid invasion of "modern life" into an otherwise very traditional and mostly nonliterate agricultural society. As a result, people belonging to the same economic and sociocultural group, often even to the same extended family, found themselves under very different sociocultural circumstances. Some of them, especially those in the remote villages, retained all aspects of a traditional, nonliterate culture and way of life. The second group included people involved in new agricultural or industrial enterprises, exposed to the new technology and means of communication, but still without access to systematic formal education. The third group comprised people who attended adult literacy courses and even teachers' colleges.

> "The research reported here," wrote Luria in 1976, "undertaken forty years ago under Vygotsky's initiative and in the context of unprecedented social and cultural change, took the view that higher cognitive activities remain sociocultural in nature and that the structure of mental activity – not just the specific content but also the general forms basic to all cognitive processes – change in the course of historical development" (Luria, 1976, p. 8).

The research methodology used by Vygotsky and Luria appeared as a synthesis of anthropological and psychological approaches. The situation of data gathering was closer to an anthropological model, with researchers conducting their study in the everyday environment, often around the evening campfire. The presentation of tasks was preceded by an unhurried conversation touching on subjects close to the daily concerns of peasants and their opinions on different matters. The tasks themselves were presented as "riddles" that were quite popular in the local culture. The presentation of "riddles" and the discussion that followed the peasants' responses resembled Piaget's method of dialogical clarification of children's concepts. As far as possible, the "riddles" themselves were cast in a culturally appropriate way and always included several possible solutions. The idea was to let the respondents answer either in a concrete and functional way that reflected their immediate everyday experience or in a verbal-logical way based on more abstractive and hypothetical reasoning.

The nature of the tasks, however, was psychological rather than ethnographic. The main target of the research was the analysis of such psychological functions as perception, memory, classification, problem-solving, and imagination. The main conclusions reached by Vygotsky and Luria on the basis of these studies were that informants who retained a traditional nonliterate culture and way of life tended to solve problems by using functional reasoning reflecting practical experiences in everyday life. They rejected the possibility of looking at classification and generalization or drawing conclusions from another (e.g., more abstractive) point of view. Exposure to modern technology and involvement in jobs based on the division of labor increased the subjects' readiness to solve problems both in functional and in verbal-logical ways. It was observed, however, that informants who did not experience formal education rather easily reverted to purely functional reasoning. At the same time, informants who received some form of formal education demonstrated a clear preference for the verbal-logical form of problem-solving. Their performance was also not different from that of urban people from Central Russia.

For example, in a study of classification and generalization, the informants were asked to group such objects as a *hammer, saw, log,* and *hatchet.* One of the informants, a peasant from a remote village who had received no formal education, responded in the following way (Luria, 1976, pp. 55–56):

PEASANT: "They are all alike. I think that all of them have to be here. See, if you are going to saw, you need a saw, and if you have to split something you need a hatchet. So there are all needed here."

RESEARCHER: "Which of these things could you call by one word?"

PEASANT: "How is that? If you call all three of them a 'hammer,' that would not be right either."

RESEARCHER: "But one fellow picked three things – the hammer, the saw, and the hatchet – and said that they were alike."

PEASANT: "A saw, a hammer, and a hatchet all have to work together. But the log has to be here too."

RESEARCHER: "Why do you think he picked these three things and not the log?"

PEASANT: "Probably he has got a lot of firewood, but if we will be left without firewood, we would not be able to do anything."

RESEARCHER: "True, but a hammer, a saw, and a hatchet are all tools."

PEASANT: "Yes, but even if we have tools, we still need wood – otherwise, we cannot build anything."

For our purposes, it is important that the informant in this episode used the words (*hammer, saw, log,* and *hatchet*) as verbal labels for material tools used in his everyday life. These words were not connected to any semantic network that would place them into such verbal categories as "tools vs. raw materials" or "made of metal vs. made of wood."

The functional approach to classification appears to be characteristic of various nonschooled populations, not just peasants from Central Asia. In our own research, we observed very similar classification reasoning in a young immigrant from Ethiopia who had no previous formal education. First, we showed him pictures of Ethiopian musical instruments and asked him whether he recognized them. The informant confirmed his familiarity with the instruments and provided their Amharic names. Then we asked him to group the pictures. The informant created several groups and explained that each group of instruments is played at specific social occasions or during specific festivities. When asked to think of a possibility of grouping the instruments differently, the informant reiterated that the instruments can be grouped only in a specified way and there is no other way of doing this. Probably the most interesting aspect of this episode was the behavior of our Ethiopian assistant and translator, who received some formal education in Ethiopia and later in Israel. He could barely restrain himself from joining the conversation, clearly indicating his awareness that, apart from social-functional grouping, these same items could be arranged into groups of string, wind, and percussion instruments (Kozulin, 1998).

Only 15 percent of illiterate peasants in the Vygotsky–Luria study were able to independently solve syllogistic "riddles" that went beyond their everyday experience, and an additional 30 percent with the help of a researcher who emphasized that the conclusion should be drawn from "his words." The results of young people who attended short-term educational courses were very different: 100 percent of them were able to solve syllogistic "riddles" that were outside their everyday experience.

In their Central Asia study, Vygotsky and Luria demonstrated that psychological functions can be understood not as natural abilities maturing in the human mind but as constructs whose emergence depends on specific sociocultural tools and activities. People from the same ethnic group and with the same childhood experience demonstrated very different responses to cognitive tasks depending on their exposure to literacy, schooling, and modern forms of work. For a variety of social and political reasons, the results of the Vygotsky–Luria study remained unavailable not only to Western but even to Russian researchers for a long time (see Kozulin, 1990; van der Veer and Valsiner, 1991). With the wisdom of hindsight, one can distinguish several questions that remained unanswered in this initial research. Vygotsky and Luria presented the process of cultural transition from traditional to modern society as a holistic phenomenon within which such sociocultural factors as the acquisition of literacy, formal classroom learning, the acquisition of new physical tools, and participation in new forms of labor were all lumped together. Each of these factors could, however, have a different impact on the construction of cognitive functions and should be investigated separately. We return later to the issue of different types of mediation; right now, however, we focus on only one of the issues pioneered in the Vygotsky–Luria study: the cross-cultural differences in the use of symbolic tools.

A Simple Grid as a Symbolic Tool

It is often assumed that while more complex cognitive functions may indeed be shaped by culture and education, more basic functions are bio-logically "prewired" and the differences in performance are between indi-viduals but not between cultural groups. Indeed, what could be more basic than the memory for positions marked on a board? Some people may have a better memory and recall all positions quicker, while others may have not such a good memory, and for them, the process of memorization will take longer. It appears that there is no place for culture in such a simple cognitive function.

This question came to the fore during our work with new immigrants from Ethiopia in Israel (Kozulin, 2008). Young immigrant adults (age range seventeen to twenty-six) came with modest previous formal educa-tional experience, ranging from no schooling at all to eight to ten years in rural Ethiopian schools. They had, however, very strong learning motiva-tion and were ready to study Hebrew, mathematics, and other subjects intensively, eight hours a day for a period of nine months with a hope to be later admitted to more prestigious vocational training programs or col-leges. The educational program that included thinking skills exercises was accompanied by cognitive testing. Here we focus on one of these tests: the positional learning task (PLT) previously used by Rey et al. (1955).

In a group version of PLT described by Feuerstein et al. (1979), and used in our study, the participants are shown a poster with a grid of twenty-five empty squares organized in a 5 × 5 pattern of columns and rows (see Figure 2.1). The evaluator then points to a specific square in each column and says "here, here, here, here, and here." In this way, five

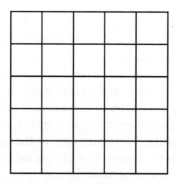

Figure 2.1   Positional learning task

positions are indicated, each one in a different column and row. After a ten-second delay, participants are asked to mark the same five positions in the 5 × 5 grid printed on their answer sheet. After the participants finish marking the positions, the procedure is repeated. Three consecutive error-less identifications of all five positions are considered to be the criterion of correct performance. Participants may then be given a different pattern of positions in the same 5 × 5 grid. If a considerable number of students in the group fail to reach the criterion level, the presentation of the same patterns continues for up to twelve trials.

Several groups of immigrant students were tested with PLT. The first group of forty-one students demonstrated that their memorization of posi-tions progressed very slowly. During the first six trials, only 9.5 percent of the students were able to reach the criterion level, and an additional 21.4 percent during trials seven to twelve, for a total of 30.9 percent in twelve trials. If one compares this to the PLT results of educated European adults (aged twenty-five to fifty-five) the difference becomes very clear: 71.4 per-cent of educated Europeans reached the criterion level during the first six trials, and 89.3 percent in ten trials.

The difference was not only in the achievement but also in the types of mistakes. The qualitative analysis of mistakes indicated that apart from such expected mistakes as marking a wrong position, immigrant students also marked the wrong number of positions (four or six, instead of five) and placed two marks in the same row or column. In addition, it was quite typical for some of them to mark the correct positions in one of the tri-als but to return to an erroneous answer during the next trial. Educated European adults on the other hand practically never made mistakes after once identifying five correct positions. Probably the most telling cultural difference in the approach to PLT was revealed by one of the immigrant students who commented that the "difficulty was with the grid." He said: "If the positions were pointed on the white board it would be easier for me. But all these lines confused me and made it more difficult."

We thought that the problem was not with immigrants' memory or spontaneous positional learning but with their lack of mastery of such a simple symbolic tool as a grid. If this hypothesis is correct then a rela-tively short intervention focusing the students' attention on the properties of the grid and its usefulness for organizing memorization should signifi-cantly improve the immigrant students' performance. This hypothesis was explored with the second group of students (N = 33) who performed the first six trials of PLT in the same way as the first group, but after that were given a brief intervention by explaining to them the structure of the grid, the role of columns and rows, and the possibility to use the properties of the grid for memorization of positions. In the first six trials, this group performed somewhat better than the first one – 18 percent of students reached the criterion level – but the main change came in trials given after intervention. An additional 60.8 percent of students reached the criterion level in trials seven to twelve for a total of 78.8 percent in the twelve trials.

These results correspond to the main thesis of the "cultural mind" approach: All human psychological functions, including those as basic as memorization of spatial positions, are shaped by sociocultural factors, the availability and appropriation of symbolic tools being among the most important. Europeans grow up in what sometimes is called a "carpentered" world: the world of straight lines, right angles, squares, and grids (Segall et al., 1966). Early on children in Europe become exposed to so-called didactic toys: squares, rectangles, and cubes made of wood or plastic. When they go to school they start using graph paper in mathematics classes and are often shown tables (columns and rows). In other words, the 90° grid is ubiquitous in European culture from the elements of architecture and interior design to the school study of geometry. The world of an Ethiopian village is very different. The houses are round, children don't have "didactic" toys that have geometric shapes, school study focuses on reading and writing, not on geometry, and graph paper is unknown. It is important to understand that for educated Europeans the grid has long ceased to be just an external feature. Because of its prominence in both the urban environment and in formal learning activities, it became internalized as one of the most basic "tools" of our perception.

Notations: Natural Development or Cultural Construction?

Sometimes, one does not need to compare the cognitive performance of students from industrial and pre-industrial societies to see how cultural and educational practices shape human cognition; it might be sufficient to compare two cultural subgroups from the same city or town. The following study is of interest not only because it provides an additional example of the role played by symbolic tools but also because it challenges a still popular idea that age-related changes in human cognition are a matter of a simple maturational process. Piaget's idea of the child's "natural" progression from one developmental stage to the next is intuitively attractive. Moreover, the development of some cognitive skills can indeed be successfully mapped on a developmental scale – unless closer attention is paid to cultural factors.

Figure 2.2   Cellphone experiment

Below we show how a cognitive process that many researchers consider to be a simple product of age-related maturation reveals its sociocultural constructive nature when studied in a sociocultural way. This particular study was triggered by the developmental research conducted by Marti and Majordomo (2003). Inspired by Piaget's theory, the authors studied textual and graphic representations of instruction generated by subjects of different ages. For their study, Marti and Majordomo used what at that time was a relatively new and attractive device: a cellular phone. That was not a modern "smartphone" but a basic cellular phone that allowed one to dial using the phone buttons (see Figure 2.2). Children and adults were first tested on their practical ability to use a cellular phone for making a call to a specified number. Then they were asked to use a sheet of paper and a pencil and make any notations necessary for instructing their peers to make a call to a specified number from the same cellular phone. The participants were forewarned that this hypothetical peer does not know how to use cellular phones.

The results of the Marti and Majordomo research indicated that the notations of younger children were not complete, the sequence of the notated actions was not accurate, and the notations constituted continuous text without drawings or other symbolic representations. Older children and adults presented a more accurate sequence of actions using a combination of schematic drawings and written text. When writing their instructions, they often presented them as a list with headings 1, 2, 3, etc. About 50 percent of the 9- and 10-year-old children used a combination of drawings and writing in their notations, while about 80 percent of the adults used such a combination. Only adults used the list format in their textual notations, while children preferred to create a continuous text.

Marti and Majordomo interpreted their findings as demonstrating an orderly age-related maturational progression of the cognitive function of representation. Younger children use only continuous writing, older children start using lists and schematic drawings, while almost all adults use a combination of schematic drawings and lists.

Our sociocultural approach, however, allowed for an alternative interpretation of these results. The subjects in the Marti and Majordomo study belonged to a modern European urban culture and were exposed to formal education. Children in this study were educated in regular public schools while the adult subjects were undergraduate psychology students. In our opinion, the changes in the symbolic means used for conveying instructions that the authors associated with age-related maturation could reflect the progressive acquisition of specific symbolic tools first at school and then at the university. One could assume that during their high school and university studies the subjects in the Marti and Majordomo study were exposed to a wide variety of notational systems, including schemas and diagrams. The experience with these symbolic tools could, in our opinion, shape their representation preferences. When confronted with cellular phone tasks they activated symbolic tools that they had already acquired and used cognitive functions developed through formal education. From this perspective, the difference between younger children and adults was not in the age-related level of representation but in the internalized experience with specific symbolic tools.

To test this hypothesis, one should find a population of educated adults who were selectively "deprived" of certain symbolic tools. If the function of representation depends only on the maturational level then all adults should use the same types of representations irrespective of their education. If, however, specific experience with symbolic tools is decisive, the performance of adults will differ depending on the type of symbolic tools they appropriated.

We replicated the cellular phone experiment with adults belonging to a specific cultural subgroup: women educated in ultra-orthodox Jewish religious schools and colleges (Kozulin, 2010). In these schools, secular subjects such as mathematics are taught only at a basic level, while science is usually not taught at all, with the bulk of the time devoted to religious subjects. At the same time, these women are familiar with such everyday communication devices as cellular phones.

Nineteen women, teachers, or teacher assistants of ultra-religious schools participated in our study. All participants confirmed that they have cellular phones and use them daily. They were told how to switch on a specific cellular phone (similar to the one used in Marti and Majordomo's study, see Figure 2.2) and how to dial numbers, and were shown the location of the "send" button. After that, the participants were asked to note on a sheet of paper instructions for making a call to a specified number. They were told that the notation was intended for a person who does not know how to use a cell phone. Subjects were asked whether they understood the instructions and their questions (e.g., "does this person know what a regular phone is?") were answered. The cellular phone was visible to the participants during their work. The target phone number was written on a whiteboard. All participants finished the task in thirty minutes.

The produced notations were analyzed according to the following dimensions: *actions* – the subjects' notations (drawings and text) were analyzed for the presence of a correct sequence of actions; *functionality* – whether the notation provides unambiguous instructions for performing all three required actions in the correct order; *type of representation* – use of drawings, a combination of drawings and writing, or text-only for conveying the instruction. A distinction was made between instructions presented as a continuous text or as a list with separate actions listed one after the other.

As expected of educated adults, all participants referred in their instructions to the three essential actions required for making cellphone calls; the sequence of actions was also correct. However, a considerable number of instructions were far from unambiguous. The predominance of purely textual instructions (68.4 percent) probably contributed to a high occurrence of incomplete or ambiguous notations. It is much more difficult to provide a complete and unambiguous description of the target actions in a textual instruction unsupported by any schematic drawings.

The main finding in our study was a lack of balance between two adult forms of representation: lists and drawings. While a considerable number of subjects (68.4 percent) used a list format in their textual instructions, only 31.6 percent used a combination of writing and drawing in their notation. So, the use of drawings by educated adults from the ultra-orthodox community was less frequent than by 9- and 10-year-old children in the Marti and Majordomo study. In our opinion, this result reflects the absence of pictorial tools in the subculture of ultra-orthodox women. At the same time, many of them used a list format in their textual instructions. This also corresponds to their previous educational and professional experience, because religious texts typically use all sorts of list notations. Lack of experience with pictorial notations may also explain a large number of mistakes made by those of our subjects who tried to use drawings. In some of the drawings, the pictorial image did not correspond to the details of the actual cellular device. For example, in one case, fifteen buttons (5 × 3) were depicted instead of the twelve (3 × 4) that existed in the displayed device. In another drawing, a group of four symmetrical operation buttons was depicted, instead of three asymmetrical ones. In yet another drawing, one nonexistent operation button was added.

From the developmental point of view, these results are paradoxical. On the one hand, adult participants perform below the level of 9-year-old children if judged by their use of schematic drawings; on the other hand, they demonstrate a perfectly adult type of text representation by using the list format. The sociocultural explanation allows us to explain this paradox. If cognitive functions are viewed as products of social and cultural experience and its internalization then there is nothing paradoxical in the situation when symbolic tools available in a given cultural environment become internalized and support a certain type of representation, while other functions remain undeveloped in the absence of experience with specific symbolic tools.

One may conclude by reiterating the classical Vygotskian claim that what appears as a natural developmental progression in a given subculture often obscures the interaction between maturational processes and sociocultural influences. It is enough to step outside this subculture for the "naturalness" of this progression to immediately disappear. Each subculture has its own set of symbolic tools appropriated and internalized by its members at different ages and in different contexts. As we have seen, even such an apparently trivial activity as using notations for giving everyday instructions is deeply influenced by the symbolic tools available to a person.

Acquisition and Internalization of Symbolic Tools

In each generation, we are confronted with the task of transmitting to children not only (and increasingly not so much) knowledge itself but the tools for acquiring, representing, organizing, and transforming this knowledge. Let us look briefly at those symbolic tools that a child is expected to become familiar with during the first four to five years of schooling at the beginning of the twenty-first century. These tools include texts (e.g., letters, words, and punctuation marks), numbers, pictures, diagrams, tables, graphs, plans, maps, and various computer interfaces (SK-12 Foundation, 2018). Of course, in industrial and post-industrial societies the majority of these tools are acquired in the context of formal education. However, even in these societies, the process of learning these tools is not that simple. First, the range of symbolic tools is rather wide, while elementary school lessons still focus mainly on literacy tools: reading and writing. Second, not many teachers recognize the difference between curricular materials presented in symbolic form and the symbolic tools (tables, graphs, diagrams, plans, formulae, etc.) themselves. The very notion of symbolic tools is usually not a part of the teachers' professional vocabulary. Third, even in industrial societies, there are considerable gaps between various socioeconomic and cultural subgroups in terms of their exposure to and practice with symbolic tools.

Though it may appear that all those symbolic tools are readily available in the child's environment, this is just one of the typical misconceptions. Even in developed countries various population subgroups have very different exposure to and understanding of symbolic tools. Just imagine a family in which the father not only shares with his son information about the results of various soccer or football games as they appear in a newspaper or on website tables but also explains to him the meaning of columns and rows of these tables. Moreover, the mother in the same family may also draw her son's attention to the table in which the forecast of temperatures and precipitation in various cities is presented. Compare this to a situation in a different family in which the bulk of communication between parents and children is oral, and such things as texts, tables, or maps never become a subject of discussion. Both children will probably become exposed to some symbolic tools in the course of their formal education. For the first of them, however, these tools may become a "natural" means of thinking and problem-solving in various life situations; for the second they may remain just a part of the material presented during the science lessons. In a sense, these symbolic media become tools only for the first child, while for the second they remain a part of the content rather than a tool. Later in this chapter, we focus on such issues as differences in availability, acquisition, and use of symbolic tools in various cultural groups.

Symbolic Tools and Problem-Solving

When students fail to solve math or science tasks it is typical to blame social factors such as poverty, poor teacher preparation, an inadequate curriculum, or outdated learning materials. What is rarely questioned is the tacit assumption that it is poor mathematical or scientific knowledge that is responsible for students' failure. But what if it is not the lack of specific content knowledge but poor general problem-solving skills that are responsible for students' lack of success? Moreover, what if it is not any type of problem-solving skills but specifically the lack of mastery of particular symbolic tools, such as tables, graphs, plans, and maps, that hinder the students' success?

The analysis of the data from international science examinations such as TIMSS (Trends in International Mathematics and Science Study) (Martin et al., 1999) and PISA (Program for International Student Assessment) (2000) demonstrated that the lack of skills related to symbolic tools may play a very serious role in students' success or failure (Zuzovsky, 2001; Zuzovsky and Tamir, 1999). It only seemed that the correct solutions to science examination tasks primarily required scientific knowledge. Actually, many of these tasks can be solved without any special scientific knowledge, just by the application of general cognitive skills. This is true not only for more open-ended PISA tasks but also for apparently more standard TIMSS tasks. For example, certain tasks that include tables do not require prior scientific knowledge regarding the parameters (e.g., density) represented in the table. It is enough to know how to work with any table so that the correct answer can be identified.

The analysis of Israeli students' mistakes in TIMSS 1999 undertaken by Zuzovsky (2001; see also Zuzovsky and Tamir, 1999) indicated that the poor results of Israeli students cannot be attributed to their lack of curricular knowledge. There was practically no difference in the results demonstrated by classes that studied the material included in TIMSS 1999 tasks and those that did not. In addition, international comparisons revealed that the Israeli school science curriculum included more topics relevant to TIMSS tasks than the curricula of the countries whose TIMSS results were better than Israeli ones. What really distinguished Israeli students was their reluctance to so much as attempt solving a problem they perceived as "unfamiliar." Zuzovsky (2001) reported that in the case of some TIMSS 1999 science tasks, more than 50 percent of the Israeli sample group did not attempt to answer. Many of these tasks just required a mastery of general symbolic tools (tables, charts, pictures, and diagrams) and an application of general problem-solving skills rather than specific disciplinary knowledge.

Let us assume that the child is confronted with a certain task, for example, a task that requires the classification of objects or events. This task can be performed using lower-level cognitive functions, such as direct memorization. The same task, however, can be solved by using a symbolic artifact (e.g., a table for organizing information). We might create one condition where the classification task is mediated by the availability of a

---

Box 2.1 Acquisition of the symbolic tool and its transformation into the inner psychological tool

Symbolic artifact → (**acquisition**) → Symbolic tool
(e.g., learning how to use a table as an external symbolic tool).

Symbolic tool → (**internalization**) → Psychological tool
(e.g., thinking about data in a "tabular" form).

---

given symbolic artifact in the child's environment. We might further create a second condition marked by the presence of an adult who is ready to teach the child how to use the table as a tool for the organization and manipulation of data. Thus, the first stage in the mediation process is the acquisition of a symbolic artifact (e.g., the table) by a child as an external symbolic tool capable of performing certain operations (see Box 2.1). Already at this stage, there are several possibilities that may eventually lead to the differential cognitive development of children. For example, a child might be born into a subculture in which such symbolic artifacts as a table are unavailable. Alternatively, even if these symbolic artifacts are available, there might be a lack of adult mentors willing to introduce the child to a table. Moreover, the sheer acquaintance with tables (as shown later) does not guarantee children's mastery of them as tools that assist students in mastering the operations of comparison and classification. Finally, if children have special needs associated with, for example, learning disorders, then even a well-intentioned teacher may still be unable to teach them the proper use of tables as symbolic tools.

These processes, however, constitute only the first, acquisitional stage of the mediation process. The second, internalization stage, requires the transformation of an external symbolic tool into an inner psychological tool. It would be a mistake to imagine that a psychological tool is just a mental copy of the external symbolic tool. When properly mediated, the core features of the table, such as its columns and rows structure and the use of superordinate concepts for headings, become internalized as a generalized psychological tool that can be used for the analysis, comparison, and classification of a wide variety of data. In other words, instead of just using a particular table, a child starts using "tabular" thinking when confronted with the task of data organization.

To investigate the role of symbolic tools in problem-solving we conducted a study with seventh-grade students (13–14 years old) using tasks that resemble those of TIMSS (see Schur and Kozulin, 2008). One of the tasks ("Stars") presented students with information about different

Table 2.1 *Stars task*

Stars	Brightness	Distance from Earth (light years)	Surface temperature (C°)	Color
A	1	8.8	10,000	blue
B	2	98.0	10,000	blue
C	3	36.0	4,000	red
D	4	62.0	10,000	blue
E	5	52.0	4,000	red

Astronomers classify stars according to their color and brightness. They are also capable of measuring the distance from Earth to each one of the stars and the temperature on their surface. In the following table, you can see these data regarding some of the stars. According to the given data, which two of the properties of the stars are most closely correlated? 1. Brightness and color; 2. Brightness and distance from Earth; 3. Distance from Earth and color; 4. Brightness and surface temperature; 5. Color and surface temperature.

parameters (brightness, color, surface temperature, and distance from Earth) of various stars and asked the question "which two properties of the stars are most closely correlated" (see Table 2.1). The students, who had never studied astronomy, were explicitly told that they didn't need any special astronomical knowledge to solve the task. Such a warning was expected to focus students' attention on the general problem-solving strategies and the use of the table as a tool for problem-solving. The result, however, was rather disappointing in terms of students' answers: Only 57 percent were able to solve the task. At the same time, this result confirmed our hypothesis about the crucial importance of such symbolic tools as a table for students' problem-solving.

The second task, "River," turned out to be even more challenging for the students. They were presented with a map that depicted a river, lake, and terrain – hills and valleys (Figure 2.3). In the task instruction, it was written that "hills and valleys are shown by means of contour lines. Each contour line indicates that all points on the line have the same elevation above the sea level." In addition, the direction to the north was indicated by the arrow with the letter N. The students were asked to answer in which direction the river is flowing – northeast, southeast, northwest, southwest – or to choose "It is impossible to tell from the map." Unlike the "Stars" task, the "River" task could not be solved without some physical and geographic knowledge, such as that the rivers flow from the higher elevation to the lower, or how the cardinal directions N, S, E, W are related to each other. At the same time, the ability to use such a symbolic tool as a contour map

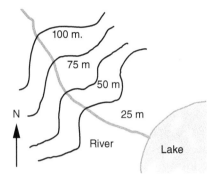

Figure 2.3   River task

and the sign for the cardinal direction to the north seemed to be crucial for solving this task. The results showed that many of the 13- to 14-year-old students were unable to use these tools and selected the answer "It is impossible to tell from the map." The overall level of correct solutions was low: 21.4 percent.

As a next step, we decided to systematically introduce these students to various symbolic tools, such as codes, diagrams, tables, and flowcharts. It is important to mention that contour maps were not among the symbolic tools taught to the students. So the students were not "taught to the task" but instead were made aware of the role played by different symbolic tools in problem-solving. The intervention was undertaken over four months for a total of twenty hours. The results of the "River" task post-test demonstrated significant improvement in students' problem-solving from 21.4 percent at the pre-test to 34.5 percent at the post-test. So, whatever content-level deficiencies associated with a poor understanding of geography and physics remained, the acquisition of various symbolic tools helped students to improve their problem-solving.

The use of external symbolic tools such as tables or diagrams is only the first stage, and is expected to be followed by the second one: internalization of these tools in the form of inner cognitive tools. A rather obvious criterion of the success of such internalization is the students' ability to choose or create symbolic tools suitable for organizing the given data or solving the problem. The ability to organize data in the form of a double-entry table was explored by Marti et al. (2011). Sixth- to eighth-grade students (ages ten to fourteen) were presented with data that showed the names, ages, and heights of twenty-five children – boys and girls. The task was to make a table that would enable us to see how many boys and how many girls are shorter than 130 cm, how many are between 130 and 149 cm, how many are between 150 and 169 cm, and how many are taller than 169 cm. The participating students were given explicit instructions to create a table with numerical data ("how many") that showed the number of boys and girls in each height category.

The first significant result of this study was that many students, despite the explicit instruction to create a table, created lists. For example, they wrote the names of the girls whose height was less the 130 cm and next to these names wrote 0–130. This confusion between lists and tables indicates that these two forms of data representation were not clearly distinct in students' minds. The second finding is related to the type of tables created by students. Though students were instructed to create tables with numerical data – the number of boys and girls in a given age interval – the majority of students included the names of children in their tables. So, the students did not distinguish between the cases table from the frequency table. In this respect, the table created by seventh-grade student Toni is rather typical. Toni organized the data in a double-entry table, with the columns corresponding to height intervals and the rows to gender. However, in the resulting cells, instead of frequencies he wrote the names and the heights of the boys and girls. In the process of completing the table he actually "lost" one of the girls who was supposed to be listed in the cell of the height interval 150–169. One can imagine that if Toni created the frequency table, it would probably be easier for him to check the numbers and realize that instead of twenty-five children he entered the data for only twenty-four.

So, we cannot but agree with Marti et al. (2011, p. 231) conclusion: "Based on the main difficulties we have identified, we propose a focused intervention in classrooms to help students internalize tables as an important tool for organizing information and solving problems."

Of course, it is not just tables that should be acquired and internalized as inner symbolic tools. In the next section, we will outline our approach to systematically teaching different symbolic tools as an integral part of the mathematics curriculum (Kinard and Kozulin, 2008).

Symbolic Tools for Rigorous Mathematical Thinking

Mathematical education finds itself in a more difficult position vis-à-vis symbolic tools than other disciplines. Other disciplines, for example, biology or physics, start with "real" objects (animals, plants, cells, water, or stones) and then use symbolic tools to organize and represent our experience with these objects. In mathematics everything is symbolic. So, on the one hand, mathematical expressions and operations offer probably the greatest collection of potential cognitive tools, but on the other because "everything is symbolic" it is difficult for a student, and often also for a teacher, to distinguish between mathematical content and mathematical tools. Of course, as we have already mentioned, in other school subjects there also exists a problem of "invisibility" of symbolic tools that are often perceived as a part of the content material. In mathematics, however, this problem is more acute because the boundary between mathematical tools and mathematical content is not very clear as the content is presented in the same symbolic language as the tools.

Before we discuss mathematically specific symbolic tools, let us pay some attention to general symbolic tools that are used in different curricular areas, including mathematics. Some of the simplest symbolic tools are signs and codes. For example, to create a list we use letters not as elements from which words are constructed but as signs of the order of statements:

A. [Statement 1]
B. [Statement 2]
C. [Statement 3], etc.

Similar to letters, numbers are often used not as an expression of quantities but as signs of the order in which information is listed. Numbers can also be used as a classification code. For example, all No. 38 buses belong to the group of buses that follow the same route. This code, however, has nothing to do with either order or quantity; bus No. 38 is not bigger than bus No. 15, and it does not appear in the street after bus No. 37.

Some educators, particularly those working in the Vygotskian tradition, claim that the mastery of general symbolic tools, such as signs, codes, and simple formulae, is the necessary prerequisite for successful elementary school learning. In their opinion, the key element in the learning process is students' awareness of their own cognitive activity. Such activity includes an exploration of the task and then a decision regarding the solution. Symbolic tools, such as signs, codes, and formulae help students to "map" the process of exploration and problem-solving. Simultaneously the process of generalization takes place. By its very symbolic nature, a sign is never a sign for one specific task but always for the entire class of tasks (Schmittau, 2004).

Let us take as an example such a part/whole schematic sign as $\wedge$.

First, this sign is used to map the exploration of the tasks that require finding parts of the whole shape (see Figure 2.4).

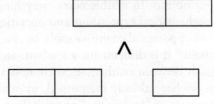

Figure 2.4   Schematic sign: ∧

Then the same sign is used with numbers:

$$8 \qquad\qquad 8 \qquad\qquad 8$$

$$\land \qquad\qquad \land \qquad\qquad \land$$

$$6 \qquad 2 \qquad 1 \qquad 7 \qquad 3 \qquad 5$$

This schematic then helps children to find the unknown, as in:

$$? + 9 = 16$$

$$16$$

$$\land$$

$$? \qquad 9$$

The whole [16] is composed of two parts. One is known (it is 9) and the other is unknown [?].

The part–whole schematic connects quantities and numbers. The relation between quantities, for example, what is the "size" of the part "?" or how much do we need to add to 9 so that we have the whole [16] becomes connected to the operation with numbers that express these quantities (e.g., $16 - 9 = ?$; $? = 7$).

The schematic sign ∧ is not specifically mathematical; it can be used in any part/whole task in geography, history, text analysis, etc. What is important is that this sign helps students to form a general cognitive model of part–whole relationships.

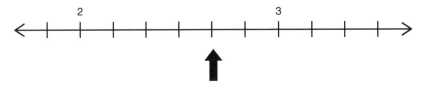

Figure 2.5 Fractions task

The acquisition of general symbolic tools is a necessary but definitely not a sufficient prerequisite of mathematical thinking. What is needed is the acquisition and internalization of more specific symbolic tools associated with mathematical activity. One of the best-known of these tools is a number line. It is typically used in the math curriculum for representing the sequence of numbers. However, the notion of representation carries with it a danger of passive acceptance rather than active use. The number line is often accepted by students as a ready-made object to be used with a limited number of standard tasks given during math lessons. As a result, the very symbolic nature of the number line and its constituent elements remains obscure.

What are the necessary symbolic elements that turn a simple line segment into a number line? There are three elements: The sign for *origin*, usually 0, the line segment selected as a *unit*, and an arrow sign indicating the *direction*. Without understanding these symbols, their roles, and relationships the active use of the number line is impossible. For example, if two numbers and a unit are given, it is possible to infer the direction and identify the point of origin even in the absence of the arrow and 0 signs. However, if only one number is given, it is impossible to infer either the direction or the origin.

The lack of understanding of the symbolic elements of the number line leads to many misconceptions (Lee and Lee, 2018). For example, misunderstanding the role of a unit leads to the erroneous counting of tick marks rather than intervals in the tasks in which the fraction should be identified using the number line. In the task shown in Figure 2.5 the student was asked to write the number (fraction) corresponding to the place on the number line indicated by the arrow. The student's answer was 2⅘ because he counted the number of tick marks between 2 and 3 rather than intervals. Because there are five tick marks between 2 and 3 and the tick mark to which the arrow is pointing is the fourth one the student assumed that the fraction should be 2⅘ (instead of 2⅔).

Sometimes the misconception is based on the confusion between the segment of the grid paper and the segment used as *unit*. For example, as

Figure 2.6   Misconceptions in fractions task

shown in Figure 2.6, the students were given a task where 5 and 7 were written on the number line, and they were asked to write 4 and 8 in their proper places. The students were expected to use the distance between 5 and 7 for determining the size of the 1 unit (which equals three grid mark segments) and to place numbers 4 and 8 three grid marks to the left and three grid marks to the right of 5 and 7 respectively. Instead, as can be seen in Figure 2.6, a student placed 4 and 8 one grid mark distance from the given numbers. This confusion of units and grid marks brings us back to the topic discussed earlier in this chapter. While discussing the PLT performance of immigrant students we mentioned the possibility that for many of them, the provided grid paper failed to serve as a tool for recalling positions. The columns and rows of the grid were perceived as a distraction rather than a useful tool. The example with the number line demonstrates a different problem associated with symbolic tools. What we see is not a lack of recognition of the possible tool function of the grid but confusion between two different symbolic tools: grid marks and the *unit* of the number line.

These examples return us to the main thesis of this section. Because of the heavy dependence of mathematical reasoning on various symbolic tools, it is essential to introduce them as tools rather than as a part of content material. Moreover, mathematical learning should start with learning about general symbolic tools, such as line segments, codes, and grids. Only after students acquire and internalize these tools and understand their possible applications is it possible to introduce mathematically specific tools without the danger of confusion between different tools.

Symbolic tools do not just help to solve mathematical problems, they also provide a "bridge" between math concepts and problem-solving. For example, using line segments to symbolically represent quantities helps to link the problems of comparison, addition, and subtraction to the concept of category or dimension of quantities. Here again, the symbolic and abstractive nature of mathematical expressions is on the one hand essential but on the other potentially misleading. In the expression $7 + 5 = 12$ nothing is told about the category or dimension of the quantities 7, 5, and 12. So, on the one hand, it is important for mathematics to allow us to

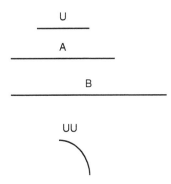

Figure 2.7   Rigorous mathematical thinking tasks

quantify and symbolically represent all possible quantities (e.g., of time, space, weight, and temperature). On the other hand, it is assumed that the students understand that the earlier expression is true only when the quantities belong to the same category or dimension: 7 meters plus 12 degrees Celsius does not produce 12 kilograms. Moreover, 7 meters plus 5 centimeters, though both of these quantities belonging to the linear space, do not result in 12 meters. So, to properly link symbolic tools to math concepts we need to train students to determine the dimension to which our quantities belong, compare them in a variety of ways, and express their relationships symbolically.

One of the possible exercises with quantities belonging to a linear space is as follows (Kinard and Kozulin, 2008, pp. 134–135):

> Draw a short horizontal line segment and encode it as U. Draw another horizontal line segment that is twice the length of U and encode it as A. Draw a third horizontal line segment that is three times the length U and encode it B. Write all possible quantitative relations between U, A, and B using the sign =.

After examining the students' answers, ask them if their conclusions will still be correct in the case of the segment UU as shown in Figure 2.7

This exercise allows us to see to what extent what usually appears as simple relationships, such as $A = 2U$, $B = 3U$, are actually comprehended and represented by students in a variety of symbolic-mathematical ways: $U = \frac{1}{2}A$; $U = \frac{1}{3}B$; $A = \frac{2}{3}B$; $B = 1\frac{1}{2}A$; $U + A = B$; $B - U = A$, etc. The question about segment UU is intended to sharpen students' understanding of the need to have quantities belonging to the same dimension, in this case "linear segments."

Symbolic Tools in Foreign Language Learning

It is not only in mathematics classrooms that symbolic tools can play a crucial role. As demonstrated by Infante and Poehner (2021), specially designed symbolic tools may also help in such a field as foreign language learning. One of the topics that is particularly difficult for some students studying English as a second or foreign language is tense and aspect. For example, what in English is expressed using the past progressive appears as past simple in some other languages, for example, Russian. In Russian the sentence "yesterday Peter was washing his car when the rain started" appears as "vchera Peter myl svoju machine kogda nachalsia dozhd'" ("Yesterday Peter washed his car when started rain"). For English language learners it is not enough to listen or read sentences that include past perfect, present perfect, or past progressive constructs to internalize the cognitive schema of these constructions. Such a schema includes three main elements: speech time, event time, and reference time. Speech time is the time when the sentence is uttered, which is "now." In the sentence about Peter, this "now" is definitely "today." The event time refers to the moment in which the speaker situates the event relative to the speech time. In the sentence about Peter, the event is located in the past: "yesterday." The reference time indicates the position of the speaker or in our case of the character (Peter) relative to the events taking place in the past: "was washing his car when the rain started." To facilitate the acquisition of English tense and aspect by English language learners, Infante and Poehner (2021) constructed graphic schematic tools that visualize different combinations of speech, event, and reference positions. So, instead of just listening to or reading texts, the learners problem-solve language tasks using a graphic schematic as a tool. For our discussion, it is not important what kind of graphic elements (rectangular shapes, color lines, or cubes) are used as symbolic tools. What is important is to provide the learner with sufficient tools to visualize different situations and facilitate their expression in the form of a proper English sentence. For the sake of illustration let us consider the tools used by Infante and Poehner (2021). Large rectangular shapes corresponding to time periods (the present, past, period before past). The "eye" sign for marking speech time ("now"), the cube whose sides symbolize different event times, for example, "past simple" (E1), "past progressive" (E2), "past perfect" (E3), and the gray chip marking the reference time.

Let us construct the "tool kit" for two sentences: "yesterday Peter washed his car" and "yesterday Peter was washing his car when the rain started." First of all, the speech time is "now" so our students should place the "eye" into the rectangular frame corresponding to the present (Figure 2.8). The

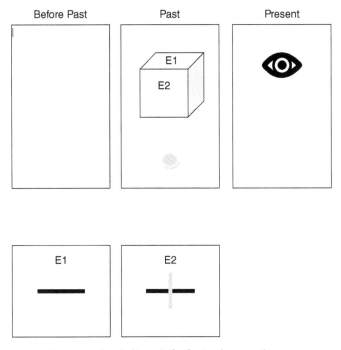

Figure 2.8   Symbolic tools for foreign language learning

word "yesterday" helps to determine that both sentences refer to the event that took place in the past. So, the cube of the event should be placed into the frame of the "past." Now the question is which side of the cube should be up. The side marked E1 symbolizes events that took place in the past and are not related to any other events. So, the cube with side E1 (past simple) up corresponds to the sentence: "Yesterday Peter washed his car." However, when an additional event took place at the same time ("the rain started") then side E2 (past continuous) should be up. The vertical red segment of this side symbolizes the co-occurrence of "washing his car" and "the rain started."

Unlike the standard language-teaching practice carried out exclusively in verbal modality and relying mainly on memorization, this example turns the language-learning practice into a mediated problem-solving experience during which students can organize their decision-making process using symbolic tools. Moreover, these tools allow teachers to mediate on different levels by indicating, for example, that the placement of the event cube is problematic, or that attention should be focused on the difference between the upper side of the cube and the selected time frame.

Conclusion

We started this chapter by pointing out the main differences between two classes of mediators: material tools and symbolic tools. While material tools are aimed at producing changes in the outside world, symbolic tools represent, organize, and transform our knowledge and objects, and events. The acquisition and internalization of symbolic tools change the way we think about the world. For example, instead of physically showing what to do with some object, we can talk about this action, write about it, or depict it graphically and schematically.

Thousands of works are written about symbolic tools in different specialized areas such as literary theory (texts), art history (pictures), mathematics (formulae), and musicology (musical notations). In many of these fields, only one representational aspect of symbols is discussed. Symbols, however, not only represent objects, processes, and events but also mediate between the world and the human mind. In the course of this mediation, they impact the way our cognitive processes are shaped. Just imagine the difference between the experience of orienting oneself in a new city being armed with such a symbolic mediator as a map or having to rely on direct vision and hearing alone. The use of a map not only changes our perception of the city but also changes the way we think about the space and our place in it. Electronic navigators might be very handy in finding specific places, but they do not provide people with cognitive tools of orientation and spatial representation. In this sense, they may be even less cognitively valuable than nonsymbolic orientation based on direct vision and hearing. In the latter case, the path from point A to point B is usually stored in our memory together with the landmarks associated with it, while the same path is completely forgotten when provided by an electronic navigator.

In the theory of the cultural mind, symbolic mediators play a very important role because the study of these mediators helps us to understand how our natural functions of perception, memory, and problem-solving become transformed into the cultural mental functions shaped by the symbolic tools available to us.

Closer attention to symbolic tools has taught us several lessons. The first of them is that different cultural subgroups use different symbolic tools, and as a result they shape their cognitive processes, even as basic as spatial memory, differently. Moreover, some of the psychological functions that at the first glance should progress developmentally irrespective of the person's experience, actually depend on the acquisition and mastery of specific tools, for example, the graphic representation of objects. The second lesson is that even in societies with formal educational systems, the teaching of symbolic tools as tools is often neglected. Tables, graphs, and formulae appear as a part of the content material instead of being learned as specific tools. We saw that many of the problem-solving mistakes made by students, for example, in international exams such as PISA and TIMSS, reflect their poor mastery of symbolic tools rather than a lack of curricular knowledge. The third lesson is that educational intervention aimed at teaching students how to identify and apply the instrumental properties of symbolic tools leads to improved problem-solving in subjects ranging from mathematics to foreign language learning. It would not be an exaggeration to say that in the school curriculum built around the concept of the cultural mind, symbolic tools may become a unifying principle connecting all subjects from art to literature and science.

CHAPTER 3

Leading Activity and Child Development

In this chapter, we explore the possibility of viewing child development not as a line of maturation milestones, not as stages of cognitive self-development (Piaget, 1950), and not as a series of emotional conflicts between the child and environment (Erikson, 1962), but as a sequence of different activities that propel child development. The starting point in this inquiry is the Vygotsky–Elkonin theory of so-called leading activities (see Elkonin, 1972; Karpov, 2005). The rather bold proposal made by Vygotsky and later developed by Elkonin and his students was that each developmental period can be associated with the activity that plays a leading role in children's lives during this period. Of course, children are involved in a large number of activities, but during a given period only one of them is crucial for the child's development. The model of leading activities is culturally specific: Leading activities are shaped by a given culture and subculture and reflect both the children's abilities and the expectations of their parents and other mentors. Socioculturally constructed leading activities serve as a motor of child development. Within each one of the developmental periods, activity-dependent cognitive and interpersonal skills lead to the formation of a new motive that corresponds to the new leading activity that becomes dominant during the next developmental period. The relationships between children and their sociocultural environment are reciprocal: The leading activities offered to children interact with children's emerging abilities and motives, while these abilities and motives are shaped and developed by the leading activities. Vygotsky, Elkonin, and their followers (see Karpov, 2005) sketched the following list of leading activities typical for industrial and post-industrial societies:

- Direct emotional contact with the caregiver – infancy.
- Joint object-centered activity – early childhood.
- Sociodramatic play – preschool age.
- Formal learning – elementary school age.
- Peer interaction – middle and high school age.
- Work activity – adulthood.

Contrary to some developmental theories (e.g., that of Piaget), which claimed the universality of developmental stages, the leading activity model is deliberately culturally specific. It does not assume that leading activities typical for industrial and post-industrial societies and their expected developmental outcomes will, for example, be the same as in preliterate societies that have no system of formal education. Later on, we investigate whether some specific features of twentieth-century Russian society became unconsciously incorporated into this culturally specific model by its authors.

It takes some cognitive effort to look at child development through the prism of leading activities. Many of the developmental phenomena described by Vygotsky, Elkonin, and their followers are well known. The problem is that because many of these developmental phenomena are so natural it is difficult to view them as engendered by specific activities. This is particularly true of infancy and early childhood. Many researchers interpreted the same phenomena as reflecting the natural development of the child and ignored the role of socioculturally constructed activities. Only when these activities are missing or a significant cultural variation takes place does their constructive nature becomes obvious.

Infancy: Direct Emotional Contact with the Caregiver

The difficulty in perceiving child development as dependent on some form of constructed activity is nowhere as obvious as during infancy. Infants appear to just go through the natural process of maturation of their body functions and sensory-motor abilities, while adults respond to infants' physical needs: food, shelter, comfortable temperature, and body hygiene. However, behind this "physiological" façade one can find a very significant psychological activity – the activity of emotional communication. Unlike the majority of newborn animals who from the very beginning have a certain degree of autonomy, human babies are totally dependent on their caregivers. One can even say that the world appears to human infants only through the activities of their caregiver who moves and carries them, brings different objects to their field of vision, controls voices and sounds coming to them, and provides them with tactile and kinesthetic stimulations. The only way in which infants can interact with the world is by establishing emotional communication with their caregivers. The successful reciprocity of this communication is the basis of infants' well-being.

One of the important aspects of such reciprocity is shared attention and pointing. There is some research evidence that around the end of the first year of life, infants already use pointing gestures to create the situation of shared attention with adults. The shared attention forms a basis for the shared interests of babies and their caregivers in objects and events. In addition, infants apparently start recognizing certain feelings and emotions that adults show regarding different situations. Adult caregivers, often spontaneously and unconsciously, create activities that promote infants' ability to develop shared feelings. Higgins (2016) suggested that shared feelings during infancy constitute the key element of this developmental period. He even went as far as to claim that the targets of shared attention and feelings can be different in different cultural subgroups. At the same time, the active-constructive element suggested in the Vygotsky–Elkonin model was still missing in Higgins' account: he described the emotional communication of infants as just taking place rather than being actively promoted by their caregivers.

If so, how can one describe the emotional interaction between caregivers and infants as an activity? First of all, such an activity is based on the very close attention that caregivers pay to infants' movements and vocalizations. Second, caregivers constantly initiate interactions with infants by establishing eye contact, smiling, bringing objects to the child's field of vision, moving objects, pointing to them, talking to infants, and touching them. Third, caregivers provide ongoing interpretations of infants' movements and their vocalization. This is a very important aspect because caregivers attribute social and psychological meaning to infants' behavior that in its initial form might be devoid of such meaning. For example, by closely observing the baby's facial expressions her caregiver may select an expression that resembles a smile and immediately label and reinforce it by smiling "in response" and adding: "Yes, Annie is smiling!"

The tendency of parents and other mentors to assign a more advanced meaning to child activity even when children themselves are still not aware of this meaning is crucial not only for emotional communication at an early age but for every developmental period. Of course, the concrete forms of such actions differ from period to period, but the principle is the same. The child's imperfect performance or understanding becomes a stepping stone for further development because adults assign to them a more advanced meaning. For example, much later in the period of formal learning teachers "translate" students' expressions (e.g., "this is a triangle") into a proper mathematical concept, while students themselves may still have a very vague understanding of the concept of geometric figures. By having a common reference with children, be it a facial expression, voice sound, or the word "triangle," adults promote children's gradual acquisition of the "adult" interpretation of these behaviors and concepts.

What happens when the activity of emotional contact with infants is insufficient or disrupted? We discussed some of the possible developmental consequences of this in Chapter 1 in the context of the role played by MLE during infancy and childhood (Klein et al., 1987). Some of the MLE criteria have a direct bearing on the activity of emotional contact with infants. One of the MLE criteria relevant here is intentionality or focusing. The caregiver makes a deliberate effort to draw the infant's attention by establishing eye contact, touching the child, placing toys within the infant's reach, and so on. All of these actions are performed with much positive emotional energy. Successful mediation of focusing also includes the caregiver's attention to the infant's reciprocal response given vocally or gesturally. An infant who receives an insufficient amount of intentionality/focusing may develop problems with imitation and coordination of actions with adults.

The issue of imitation is crucial for some infants with special needs. As shown by Feuerstein et al. (2015), infants with Down syndrome don't imitate the facial expressions of caregivers with the same ease as infants who have typical development. While for "regular" infants it is sometimes enough to see a certain facial expression only a few times before they are already capable of imitating it, infants with Down syndrome remain "unimpressed." Moreover, their parents quickly give up because of the lack of reciprocity from the side of the child. Thus the vicious circle is formed by "no response" from the side of the child leading to "no initiative" from the side of the caregiver. Feuerstein demonstrated that infants with Down syndrome may require ten times more exposure to a certain facial expression before they imitate it and that their parents should be aware of this and adjust the quantity of mediation to the needs of their children.

The second criterion of MLE relevant to the activity of emotional contact is the mediation of meaning or "exiting." This criterion is directly related to the activity of emotional contact because it emphasizes the emotional and energetic value of the actions of children and adults – "this is why we do this!" Through the mediation of meaning, infants on the one hand are taught the language of emotions, while on the other hand they see how certain actions are accentuated by a certain emotional expression. The emotional meaning can be achieved by vocal emphasis, gestures, or words. Infants who are deprived of the mediation of meaning may later suffer from the dissociation between actions and their motives. On the clinical level, this is often observed in children with an autistic spectrum disorder. The question remains of course whether the initial autistic impairment prevents these infants from fully benefiting from the mediation of meaning provided by their caregivers, or whether the caregivers' lack of attention to the special mediational needs of these infants results in a serious dissociation between emotions and actions at a later age.

As with every leading activity, the activity of emotional contact with caregivers has two functions: It develops the most important psychological functions during the given developmental period and it creates the necessary prerequisites for the transition to the next period. The activity of emotional contact is responsible for the development of coordination between mother and child in what concerns their vocalization and gaze movement (Northrup and Iverson, 2020). Coordination and imitation are fundamental abilities that during the later developmental periods will continue to serve as a basis for children's learning. The activity of emotional contact also contributes to the development of children's speech and sensory-motor activities promoted and supported by caregivers.

In a more general sense, the activity of emotional contact creates the necessary context for the mediation of transcendence or expanding. According to Klein et al. (1987), infants are capable of learning how to look beyond "here-and-now" situations. Caregivers are expected to connect the current interactive episode with the past and future, the current emotion to the same emotion displayed earlier, the current activity (e.g., bathing) to the wider range of notions (e.g., water, soap, cleanliness, fresh clothes). Through these activities, the caregivers provide infants with interpretations that go beyond the infants' current abilities but pave the way for their future development. For example, after bathing the child the caregiver may say: "Now Alan wants to put on a fresh pajama." Of course, Alan as an infant still does not understand the connection between bathing and fresh clothes, but by attributing this decision to him ("Alan wants") the caregiver prepares the child for the next developmental period during which children will actively use adults for facilitating activities initiated by children themselves. The lack of mediation of transcendence at an early age may result in what Feuerstein et al. (2015) call the episodic grasp of reality. Instead of spontaneously connecting a new experience with previous ones and projecting it into possible future events, the experiences of children who were deprived of the mediation of transcendence remain episodic and disconnected.

All functions developed during the period of direct emotional contact create the basis for the transition to the next developmental period: the period shaped by the joint object-centered leading activity. The caregivers continue to play a very important role during this period, but this role is different. If during the first period the caregiver's presence, voice, gaze, and touch were of primary importance while specific objects were secondary, now objects come to the fore while the caregiver's role is to facilitate children's interactions with these objects.

Toddlers and Young Children: Object-Centered Joint Activity

In the Vygotsky–Elkonin developmental model (Elkonin, 1972), the order of transitions is always between two poles: social-emotional and objective-operational (see Table 3.1). Emotional contact with caregivers prepares the ground for the children's transition to the object-centered activity. By the end of the object-centered activity period the greater facility with objects, both physical and verbal, will create conditions for the transition to the next leading activity that belongs to the social-emotional group: the period of sociodramatic play.

The issue of the socioculturally constructed nature of toddlers' activities is very contentious. After all the major achievements of children during this age period, the development of speech and manipulation with objects appear very natural. All children, except those with special needs (e.g., autism), seem to spontaneously acquire native language and the age-appropriate sensory-motor skills that allow them to become actively engaged in both practical (e.g., washing, eating) and playful activities. However, in digging a bit deeper the naturalness of these acquisitions turns out to be less obvious.

Let us start with the phenomenon that received the popular name the "30 million word gap." The name comes from the main finding of the Hart and Risley (1995) study that showed that by the age of four, the most advantaged American children had heard 30 million more words addressed to them than the least advantaged children. This gap then

Table 3.1 *Leading activities and the periods of child development*

Period	Social-emotional leading activity	Objective-operational leading activity
Infancy	Direct emotional contact with the caregiver	
Early childhood		Joint object-centered activity
Preschool age	Sociodramatic play	
Elementary school age		Formal learning
Adolescence and youth	Peer interaction	
Adulthood		Work activity

strongly correlates with school achievement. The "most advantaged" in this context are children whose parents are better educated (e.g., has a college or graduate degree), and as a result on average they have a higher SES. Moreover, not only do the advantaged children hear more words, but they also hear more varied language forms and are engaged in more conversational turns with their parents. So, it is not just the number of words but the quality of verbal activity that distinguishes these families. Of course, being from a low-SES family does not automatically mean that the child would not be engaged in meaningful verbal activity. On the contrary, it was shown that in low-SES families the quality of parent–child verbal activities is strongly correlated with the later language development of the child.

For example, in the study conducted by Hirsh-Pasek et al. (2015) mothers of 2-year-old children from low-SES families were observed while they played with their children using the contents of three boxes. In the first box there was a picture storybook, in the second box a toy stove and cooking accessories, and in the third box a simple dollhouse with a few moving parts and figures. Mothers' interactions with their children were rated for fluency and connectedness. In other words, the balance between partners' contributions, how the partners negotiated taking turns, and how smoothly the interaction progressed. The second rating was of the children's sustained attention to shared objects, events, and symbols while playing with the parent. Symbols included both words and symbolic gestures. For example, as the child and parent played together with the dollhouse, the child produced a verbal label ("baby") and a symbolic gesture (placing head on hands to indicate sleep) as the mother placed the figure in the bed. The child might also demonstrate comprehension of the mother's language by following a verbal direction ("put that baby to sleep"). The third rating was the frequency and quality of routines and rituals that occurred during shared activities. These included the use of familiar play routines ("my turn–your turn") or such scripts as "book reading" or "bedtime." Sometimes the rituals included a set sequence of activities, for example, the parent and child "prepared" breakfast and then "ate" it and sometimes even had an explicit connection to a prior event ("Remember when we made blueberry muffins?").

The study by Hirsh-Pasek et al. (2015) showed that the quality of mother–child interaction at the child's age of twenty-four months had a strong impact on the child's language performance at the age of thirty-six months. It was further shown that the quality of early communication adds to the prediction of later language outcomes over and above the parent's general warmth, sensitivity, stimulation, and the number of the parent's words. It is not just the general warmth that was important in early infancy but the quality of structured interaction between adults and toddlers that play a major role in promoting children's verbal functions during this period. Hirsh-Pasek and her colleagues hypothesized that the key to the effectiveness of parent–child interactions lies in providing scaffolds for the child's engagement with shared objects, the sharing of communicative routines, and the mutual negotiation of the flow of the ongoing interaction. "When words are introduced within parent-supported shared activities, a child can learn their meaning and practice their use. Without sufficient scaffolding, parents' words might flow by like background noise, with no impact on child learning" (Hirsh-Pasek et al., 2015, p. 1081).

The same line of reasoning emerged in the study of Michnick Golinkoff et al. (2019), who argued that what is important is not the total number of words uttered in the children's environment but the words included in the interactive routines that keep children's attention by providing them with useful contextual cues. A child sitting in a high chair who hears, for example, "Juice. You like your juice?" is receiving input that is contextually specific and related to a certain routine. On the other hand, mere exposure of a child to adults' decontextualized talk is much less effective.

These studies, though they are not based on the concept of leading activities, lend strong support to the leading activity concept. It is a joint object-related activity of adults and children, rather than children's spontaneous development or "osmotic" learning, that promotes children's verbal development during this developmental period. Language, however, is not the only function to develop at this age.

During this period children learn how to solve problems and coordinate their actions with adults. For example, children become engaged in shared practices that include helping another person who is having difficulty completing a goal, such as an adult who accidentally dropped a play object on the floor. Children become more skillful in coordinated play, the one where success requires that each participant performs a different function (e.g., one person holds the container in place while the other retrieves the object). It is also during this period that children engage with others in a more coordinated turn-taking manner, such as waiting their turn and timing what they do to be responsive to what's happening with their partner.

In a more general sense, what emerges during the period of object-directed leading activity are shared practices. Probably nowhere does the essence of shared practices become more conspicuous than in the situation of "scaffolded" problem-solving. This is how the activity of scaffolding is described in the much-quoted study of Wood et al. (1976). The task given to the children was to construct some sort of pyramid using square blocks of wood of different sizes that could be linked to each other using dowels. This task is usually too difficult for young children because it involves selecting the blocks according to their size and shape, assembling them in a specific sequence, orienting the assembled parts, and putting them on top of each other so that the structure of the pyramid is achieved. If one assumes that children's problem-solving reflects only their own abilities, then younger children still don't have the relevant abilities for solving this task. If, however, children's problem-solving is viewed from the perspective of leading activities, then the question is different, namely in what kind of activity should the children become engaged so that their emerging but still immature abilities can be revealed and supported?

Wood et al. (1976) suggested that this should be an activity of joint problem-solving during which adults provide children with "scaffolds" that support children's emerging problem-solving strategies and skills. "Scaffolds" of course can be of various levels of concreteness, from very general suggestions such as "why don't you try to put some blocks together" to very specific verbal instructions about the assembly or physical demonstration. Wood and his colleagues showed that the effectiveness of "scaffolding," namely the ability of children to progress in problem-solving with the help of prompts given by adults, depended first of all on the "contingency" of these prompts. The prompt is "contingent" when its selection is based on the child's response to the previous prompt. When the previous prompt was insufficient, the adult may try a more concrete "scaffold," but when the child succeeds in using the previous prompt then the adult may let the child be more responsible for his/her next step.

The selection of "scaffolds" in the joint problem-solving activities of course depends on the nature of the task, but it also depends on the interactive style of the adults. This style appears to be culturally specific. To elaborate on this aspect of joint problem-solving further we need to refer again to some of the MLE criteria presented in Chapter 1 and discussed in the previous section. In a series of studies, Tzuriel (1996, 1997) explored which parameters of mothers' MLE are more prominent in the interaction with their children depending on mothers' SES and cultural affiliation. Tzuriel demonstrated that in general the higher the SES level of the mothers, the higher their MLE score. Three criteria of MLE – transcendence, mediation of meaning, and mediation of the feeling of competence – turned out to be particularly sensitive to the mothers' SES status. The criterion of transcendence captures the mediation of "going beyond the here-and-now situation." Mediation of meaning involves explanations regarding the motivation for performing particular operations, while mediation of feeling of competence provides children with positive feedback together with an elaborate explanation of why children's actions were appropriate. It turned out that the MLE criterion as transcendence is so SES-sensitive that significant differences in the amount of mediation of transcendence were found not only between high- and low-SES mothers but even between high- and medium-SES mothers.

Tzuriel (1997) also showed that there appear to be some cultural preferences for various MLE parameters in mother–child joint activities. In his study of mother–child interaction in immigrant families from Ethiopia both traditionally oriented (weaving, handicrafts) and Western-oriented (analogy problem-solving) tasks were used. Tzuriel discovered that different parameters of mediation come to the fore depending on the type of task. For example, traditional activities elicited higher amounts of mediation of meaning and transcendence than Western tasks, but the amount of intentionality was lower in traditional situations.

The comparison of mediational styles of Ethiopian and native Israeli mothers demonstrated that they emphasized different aspects of mediation. Intentionality and regulation of behavior were more prominent in the mediation of Ethiopian mothers, while mediation of the feeling of competence was more often displayed by Israeli mothers. Moreover, while for the native Israeli sample, the amount of MLE exhibited during the mother–child interactions predicted their children's performance in the cognitive inferential reasoning test, this connection was absent for the Ethiopian sample. In other words, the aspects of MLE captured by the MLE observational scales were predictive of the ability to learn problem-solving tasks in native Israeli children but not in Ethiopian children.

The latter finding reminds us about the sociocultural stance of the theory of leading activities. Not only might the activity itself, such as joint problem-solving, have a leading status in one culture but not in the other, but the parameters of parental mediation during the joint problem-solving may also be culturally specific. The transition from one culture to another can be operationalized not only through the change in symbolic tools, as discussed in Chapter 2, but also through becoming involved in different types or sequences of leading activities and mediations that support these activities.

If we remain, however, with the leading activities model applicable to industrial and post-industrial societies, we should conclude this section with a summary of the developments that are central to the period of joint object-related activities and the role they play as prerequisites for the transition to the next period. During the period of joint object-related activities children comprehend the physical world – the world of objects and actions – as a world infused with human cultural meanings. At the beginning of this period a physical object, let us say a spoon, was just a physical object of a certain shape, material, and weight that can be used for a wide range of actions, from creating noise by banging it, to throwing it or moving other objects by pushing them. A spoon also appeared as a part of the feeding activity, but this function had no privileged position among other uses. By the end of this developmental period, a spoon ceased to be just a physical object and acquired a clear cultural meaning firmly embedded into the joint activities with adults around the dinner table.

In part, this happened because exactly during this period two of the major lines of a child's cognition become intertwined. The nonverbal object-oriented problem-solving of children becomes intertwined with children's communicative speech. In Vygotsky's (1934/2012, p. 89) words: "In the speech development of the child, we can with certainty establish a pre-intellectual stage, and in his thought development, a pre-linguistic stage ... At a certain point, these two lines meet, whereupon thought becomes verbal, and speech rational."

Instead of being just a tool of communication, language also becomes a tool of thinking and problem-solving, while problem-solving, instead of being restricted to physical manipulation, moves to the inner, verbal plane of the child's thought. The child's understanding of the world of physical objects as a "human world" infused with cultural meanings and the ability to communicate about this world verbally creates the necessary prerequisites for the transition to the next developmental period. If the period of joint object-related activities was objective-operational, the next period is social-emotional. For example, in the period of object-related activities, the toy truck is important to a child because of its culturally meaningful physical properties: It has the same parts as a real truck and it can be moved in more or less the same way as real trucks move. During the next period, the emphasis is on the child playing the role of the truck driver. The toy truck becomes just a physical prompt for the social role-playing as a truck driver.

Preschool Age Period: Sociodramatic or Make-Believe Play

Sociodramatic or make-believe play can be defined as an activity during which children become involved in an imaginary situation, assume and play certain roles, and follow a set of rules determined by those specific roles (Karpov, 2005). It is important to remember the difference between specific play actions that may take place during several developmental periods and sociodramatic play as a central leading activity of this specific period. It is true that younger children demonstrate some elements of role play, and that the adults may act playfully by assuming some imaginary roles, but it does not mean that make-believe play is the leading activity during early childhood or adulthood. To have the status of leading activity, make-believe play should be responsible for promoting the most important developmental innovations of the given age period and creating prerequisites for the transition to the next period: the period of formal learning.

What, then, are the most important innovations during the preschool period? The first of them is imagination. It is sometimes assumed that children's make-believe play is the application of children's pre-existing power of imagination. The theory of leading activities proposes the "reversed" relationships: Instead of being the precondition of make-believe play, children's greater power of imagination is perceived as its consequence (Bodrova and Leong, 2015, 2019). In other words, it is through the activity of sociodramatic play that children develop their imaginative abilities: the abilities that will serve them not only in make-believe but also in formal learning situations.

The second innovation is planning and self-regulation. To have a make-believe play, children need to select the role, choose physical prompts that support it, and follow the rules, usually dictated by the "adult" role they are playing. Unlike simple manipulation with attractive toys typical in the previous period, make-believe play cannot be purely spontaneous but requires a certain amount of planning. There is no play without rules and following these rules children gradually increase their self-regulation abilities.

The third innovation is the ability to look at situations from a different point of view. This ability is particularly important because in Piaget's (1950) theory the preschool age is portrayed as almost completely dominated by the child's egocentricity and inability to perceive objects or situations from different perspectives. Here we can see the main theoretical difference between Piagetian and other "naturalistic" approaches to child development, on the one hand, and the cultural mind approach, on the other. In Piaget's and other similar theories, children's difficulties with decentration appear as an inevitable stage in child development, the stage that should simply pass so that the child becomes less egocentric. In the theory of the cultural mind, the same period appears as a period when, through the leading activity of make-believe play, children actively master the skill of decentration and the assumption of different positions. Make-believe play is not an egocentric phantasy of children but is, on the contrary, a playful way of mastering different roles and, probably more importantly, acquiring the ability to switch these roles. The combination of imagination and switching roles becomes crucial during the period of formal learning when children have to imagine situations presented in literary and historical texts and perceive them from the point of view of different characters. On a personal level, school-age children will have to constantly switch their roles as sons and daughters to those of students and vice versa.

The fourth innovation is an increased aptitude for symbolization. At the beginning of this developmental period, children's make-believe play is still connected to the physical properties of the prompts. For example, children may need some play food to pretend they are at the restaurant. Then they will use prompts that are different in appearance but with which the same operation can be used as with the "real" object (e.g., a paper plate symbolizing a pizza). Finally, closer to the end of this period symbolization shifts from objects to speech and gestures. For example, the child in the role of a "customer" in a pretend restaurant indicates by a gesture that she is eating (Bodrova and Leong, 2019). The ability to assign a certain meaning to an object that has no physical resemblance to its referent is a major step toward symbolic activities that constitute the basis of school learning (see Chapter 2). School learning is all organized around text-based realities, while the properties of texts have no physical connection to sounds or concepts. So, when a child assigns the meaning of a horse to the long stick in a play situation, such a child is making the important step toward such symbolic action as using the letters h-o-r-s-e to stand for an animal that has no physical affinity to these marks.

Now let us consider the following make-believe play episode reported by Laura Berk (Berk and Winsler, 1997) and check which of the elements of social-emotional play as a leading activity can be detected during this episode.

The episode starts with one of the two girls pulling a small wagon in which the second girl (T) is sitting. "Stop the bus!" shouts T and jumps out. T goes to the corner where Mrs. B is seated. Mrs. B addresses T and asks her where she has been and where she has traveled on the bus. T answers that she "went for a ride" and Mrs. B further inquires if the girl indeed went for a ride. T responds to this inquiry by explaining that she went to the store. So, Mrs. B asks what T has bought in the store.

T whispers in response and Mrs. B exclaims: "Oh, Christmas candy! Where is this Christmas candy?" T replies that she left it on the bus. Mrs. B suggests that when the bus driver comes back T will probably be able to get the candy back.

As is quite typical for make-believe play situations taking place in children's homes, adults, in this case Mrs. B, are actively involved in children's play by "confirming" the imaginary situation and encouraging its elaboration. So, in this episode, Mrs. B. promptly picked up T's imaginary claim that the girl traveled by bus and created a further opening for T to state that she went to the store. Mrs. B also made an important remark by asking "Where is this Christmas candy?" This remark confronted T with an opportunity to either use one of the available objects as a prompt for candy or, as the girl chose, give an imaginary explanation that required no prompts: "I left it on the bus." Mrs. B also augmented the imaginary situation by adding such a socially meaningful character as a bus driver. In this way, an almost realistic story of T's travel to the store was created through a cooperative effort between T and Mrs. B.

After checking the role of an adult, let us check the girl's make-believe actions and the material prompts used for them. What is distinctive in this episode is that material prompts play a relatively minor role in the imaginary situation. While the ability of a small wagon to move on wheels is important because it turned the wagon into a suitable substitute for a bus, the rest of the situation was purely imaginary and at the same time firmly anchored in social reality. Everything that the girl said about her travel to the shop existed only on a verbal-imaginary plane without any need for prompts. Apart from telling about her imaginary travel to the shop, T apparently also enacted another element of social-interpersonal routines that she acquired: She whispered about the Christmas candy as if this information was privileged and highly important. As already mentioned, the verbal-imaginary quality of T's make-believe play probably reached its peak in T's rejection of the possibility of choosing a physical prompt for candy and opting instead for yet another verbal-imaginary explanation of leaving it on the bus. Based on this episode we may hypothesize that T must be pretty advanced in her make-believe abilities and quite soon will be able to imagine situations on the purely verbal plane.

Now let us consider which abilities developed during the period of sociodramatic play will be essential for the transition to the next developmental period: that of formal education. This question brings us to an important question of school readiness. Usually, school readiness is evaluated by comparing the children's performance in the areas of language, numeracy, literacy, problem-solving, self-regulation, and social intelligence in kindergarten and elementary school (Pace et al., 2019). It is almost self-evident that children who perform better in a certain area, for example, numeracy at the kindergarten age, and who receive adequate schooling, will also perform at a good level in school, especially since the tests used at these two data points are the same or very similar.

The theory of leading activities, however, views school readiness in a different light. First of all, as emphasized by the very name "leading activities," children's readiness for the transition to the new period is perceived as a result of some systematic activities rather than simple maturation and accumulation of skills. That is why the concept of leading activities has been used for the development of intervention programs deliberately constructed to prepare preschoolers for the transition to formal education. Two of these programs Tools of the Mind (Bodrova and Leong, 2007) and Keys to Learning (Dolya, 2007) are discussed in some detail in Chapter 5 in the context of cognitive education. What is important for us now is to see how school readiness is interpreted in these programs.

The mainstream understanding of children's school readiness focuses on children's specific skills, such as literacy and numeracy. The leading activities approach focuses instead on the development of children's much broader abilities such as imagination, especially on the verbal-cognitive plane, the ability to symbolically represent objects, situations, and relationships, and self-regulation. These broader abilities will facilitate children's acquisition of more specific skills such as literacy and numeracy but on a much wider basis. Some of the research conducted with the Tools of the Mind program (Diamond et al., 2007) showed that children who were taught this broader program demonstrated better literacy gains than children in a comparison group who were taught more specific literacy skills. Of course, focusing on the broader cognitive and learning abilities promoted by the leading activity programs at the preschool age also corresponds to a very special understanding of the goals of elementary school education formulated by this theory. This understanding of the leading activity during the elementary school period is the topic of the next section.

Elementary School Age: Formal Learning as a Leading Activity

At the first glance, it appears to be rather trivial to state that formal learning constitutes the leading activity at the elementary school age. After all, children of this age spend a considerable part of their waking hours either in school or preparing homework assignments. Yet the way the theory of leading activities defined the developmental goal of this period is very different from typical descriptions of school learning. Usually, elementary school learning is defined as an acquisition of such skills as reading, writing, and operation with numbers which then help children to accumulate curricular knowledge in literature, history, mathematics, etc. It is assumed that the acquisition of literacy and numeracy skills is achieved with the help of learning abilities already possessed by children. It is sometimes tacitly, sometimes explicitly stated that learning during this period is essentially the same type of learning as during the preschool period or in high school, while only the content is different. Learning after all is a universal human ability. So, it is often argued that at the beginning of formal education children's learning abilities are applied to relatively simple material which then becomes more complex and challenging. For example, first letters are learned, then words; first numbers are learned, then algebraic formulae. This typical understanding of school learning is based on the assumption that learning is more or less the same in all areas of life – in school and out of school.

In the theory of leading activities (Karpov, 2005) an important distinction is made between learning as a generic ability and formal learning as an activity particular for the elementary school age. Learning as a generic ability appears throughout the lifespan as a supporting element in various contexts such as play, practical activity, and interpersonal interactions. Moreover, the theory of leading activities claims that only during the elementary school period does formal learning possess the necessary quality for leading children's development. This quality is achieved when the "meeting" takes place between children's sensitivity toward learning and the instructional intentions of their teachers. During the next developmental period, that of adolescence and youth, formal learning ceases to be the leading activity though students continue to attend school.

The claim about the particular developmental role of formal education is culture-specific. It is obviously inapplicable to child development in societies that don't have a system of formal education. Moreover, many schools in industrial or post-industrial societies fail to realize the developmental potential of formal education simply because they do not see it as a factor contributing to child development. Development in these school systems is perceived as a more or less natural process of physical and mental maturation while education is seen as a provider of specific skills and knowledge. The theory of leading activities, on the contrary, claims that formal education plays a powerful role in child development. This claim stems from the more general premise of the theory of the cultural mind that human cognition and learning are shaped by sociocultural practices and that even such basic functions as perception, attention, memory, and problem-solving of educated children will be different from those who had no access to formal education. What is very important, however, is how formal educational activities are shaped. Depending on their structure and goals their developmental impact will be different.

Because the theory of leading activities has been developed by a particular group of Russian researchers some of its features bear a cultural imprint of this group. For example, Zuckerman (2014) explicitly stated that their version of formal learning aims to develop a child exclusively as a reflective self-sufficient learner. All other aspects of child development, such as a feeling of happiness, obedience to authorities, or moral rectitude are left outside the leading activity model and are expected to be developed in the social and family contexts outside the school. Even terminologically this theory preferred to call their version of formal education "developmental education" and to make a clear distinction between generic learning and specially constructed "learning activities."

Like many other innovative approaches, developmental education started with a critique of the more traditional approaches to elementary school learning that mainly ignored children's reflection and metacognition. These traditional approaches assumed that all instructional models should be provided by the teachers and that all tasks should have explicit instructions and only one correct solution. Students were not supposed to request proof for the statements made by an authority figure (e.g., teacher), and diverse opinions were of little value because "if I am right, all others should be wrong." The proponents of developmental education claimed that: "It is distressfully difficult to counterbalance and root out such habits in the middle school; it is much easier to lead the elementary school children directly toward the reflective habits of mind" (Zuckerman, 2004, p. 11).

So, developmental education was built on the idea of the early introduction of children to reflective practices to prevent the development of bad habits. Already in the first grade, children are taught to critically explore tasks presented by the teacher and check for possible "traps" that make finding one correct answer problematic. Children are also introduced to some basic symbolic tools, such as line segments to represent objects' parameters (e.g., length, width, volume) and the signs of equality ($=$), greater than ($>$), and smaller than ($<$) to be used in formulae that expresses the relationships between objects' parameters.

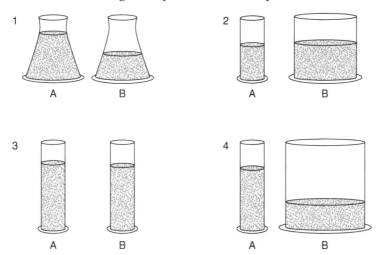

Figure 3.1   Developmental education task for first-grade children

Let us examine how the following task (Figure 3.1) is presented to first-grade children in the developmental education classroom (Alexandrova, 1998). The children are shown the pictures and are asked to compare the amount of liquid in each pair of vessels, they are encouraged to create schematic representations of the tasks and to write the formula of the relationships. They are also warned that there might be a "trap" in one of the tasks. It is easy to see that the tasks themselves are very similar to the conservation tasks used by Piaget and his followers for detecting the preoperational thinking of children. However, in the developmental education classroom, the goal of these tasks is not to identify children's "spontaneously incorrect" answers but to lead children to "nonspontaneously correct" solutions.

To accomplish this goal, the children's attention is drawn to several parameters of each one of the objects, such as shape, size, and level of liquid. Children schematically represent these parameters by drawing line segments and writing formulae. For example, two vessels in task 3 are represented by line segments of the same length while the comparison of the amount of liquid are represented by the formula: A = B. Children are asked to think about what is similar and what is different between tasks 1 and 3. They come to the conclusion that in both tasks the pair of vessels are of the same shape and size, but while in task 3 the level of liquid in the two vessels is the same, in task 1 the level in 1A is higher than in 1B. The children then are led to the operation of inferential reasoning that helps them to reach the following conclusion: If two vessels have the same shape and size and in one of them the level of liquid is higher than in the other one, then the amount of liquid in the first one is greater than in the second.

The children are then encouraged to check if the same principle applies to tasks 2 and 4. The children discover that the principle does not work because the initial condition of two vessels having the same shape and size is absent here: The vessels have different shapes and sizes. So, children are led to compare tasks 2 and 4. This comparison leads them to the conclusion that while in task 2 the levels of liquid in the larger (2B) and smaller (2A) vessels are the same, in task 4 both the vessels and the levels are different. For task 2 children conclude that if the level of liquid in the two vessels is the same but one of the vessels is larger than the other one, then the amount of liquid in the larger vessel is greater than in the smaller one. Finally, children are confronted with a difficult problem represented by task 3. One of the major goals of this lesson was to teach children how to detect a possible "trap," namely the task that does not have sufficient information for finding an unequivocal solution. The activity of finding "traps" serves an even more general purpose of preparing children for always investigating whether the tasks they confront have no correct solutions, one correct solution, or several correct solutions. Later children will learn how to identify and add the missing information so that the task that was originally impossible to solve becomes solvable.

The schematic representation of the task's properties constitutes one of the key elements of the developmental education curriculum. Already in the first grade children are taught to think about the problems not in terms of objects but in terms of their symbolic representations (see Chapter 2). Only the essential properties of the tasks (e.g., shape, size) are captured in these representations. During this early stage of formal education, children are introduced to the notion of essential vs. superficial and to the operation of abstracting the essential parameter. The symbolic representations of the essential parameters of the task first appear as visual schematics, such as segments of lines or strips of paper, and then become an inner symbolic mental representation of the problem and the methods of its solution. In a sense, the typical sequence of teaching "first numbers and only later algebraic formulas" is reversed. Children first learn the relationships of equal, greater, and smaller and how to represent them symbolically ($=$, $>$, $<$) and only later add the numerical values to these "algebraic" representations.

The schematic representation of tasks and the methods of their solution constitutes only one of the strategies of developmental education (Zuckerman, 2004). The second strategy is collaborative learning. The developmental goal of this strategy is to make children aware of the point of view of others on the tasks and phenomena that appear to be "obvious" to children themselves. This in part is achieved by asking older (e.g., fourth-grade) children to teach some topic to younger (e.g., first-grade) children. Being confronted with the fact that something that seemed to be self-evident to the fourth-grade "teachers" is far from being such to their first-grade "students," forces the fourth graders to perform meaningful reflective actions. The resulting enhancement of the children's metacognitive skills appears to be similar to those reported by Tzuriel and Shamir (2007). In Tzuriel and Shamir's study, older children were instructed on how to use the criteria of mediated learning (see Chapter 1) for teaching younger children. One of the interesting results of this study was that not only did younger "students" improve their problem-solving skills but their older "teachers" also improved their own learning and problem-solving skills: the skills that required meaningful reflection.

An additional benefit of collaborative learning is the development of children's need for justifying their solutions in front of their peers. Children in the developmental education classroom become accustomed not only to voicing their opinion (correct/incorrect) regarding the solutions presented by their peers standing at the blackboard, but also demanding an explanation. Of course, such a peer-learning activity is not spontaneous but is firmly orchestrated by the teachers, who select which of the students' solutions should be presented and when, so that such a presentation leads to the desired learning outcome.

The third strategy widely used in developmental education classrooms is children's self-assessment. This strategy corresponds to the developmental goal of self-evaluation as a part of reflective thinking. Many young but also not-so-young students perceive the evaluation of their school achievement as a subjective action on the part of their teachers who either appreciate them or not. Teaching the techniques of self-assessment that include jointly creating the evaluation scales, determining the "weight" of each evaluation task, and designing the evaluation procedures leads children to understand that evaluation is not a subjective act of the teacher but a procedure based on some objective properties of both the tasks and the student's responses. The assessment results are thus demystified because children become actively involved in selecting the tasks, establishing their "weight," and determining how the scoring is done. In this sense developmental education was a pioneer in the field of self-assessment that later became a part of the formative assessment paradigm (Black and William, 2010, p. 88): "For formative assessment to be productive, pupils should be trained in self-assessment so that they can understand the main purposes of their learning *and thereby grasp what they need to do to achieve.*"

As mentioned earlier in this section, the lessons of the developmental education curriculum are targeted not so much at the development of specific curricular skills as to shaping the children's habits of mind. Of course, the curriculum-specific skills and knowledge are not ignored, but they become developed in the context of introducing children to conceptual learning and the "big ideas" in a given curricular field. The criterion of success is the children's ability to grasp the general principle and apply it to the tasks that have not been previously given in the classroom. If children acquire the habits of conceptual reasoning in elementary school they will be ready to face more complex curricular tasks in middle and high school.

Let us check how this approach works in practice using as an example such a "big idea" as proportionality (Vysotskaya et al., 2021). Proportionality tasks are difficult for students of different ages because they require taking into account and coordinating two quantities of different types. For example, the following problem proved to be difficult for many American students: "Alan opened a faucet A and collected 6 liters of water in his bucket in 20 minutes. Ben opened a faucet B and collected 3 liters of water in his bucket in 10 minutes. Were the faucets dripping equally fast or was one dripping faster than the other"?

Some students claimed that faucet A was dripping slower because "it took more time," others claimed that A was dripping faster than B because both the time and the amount of water were greater for this faucet. One of the possible explanations for this difficulty is that students take each one of the parameters, time, or the amount of water separately, instead of coordinating them and using such a compound unit as liter/minutes (Lobato and Ellis, 2010).

To provide an early conceptualization of proportionality the adherents of the developmental education curriculum proposed to introduce 7-year-old children to the concept of the compound unit or "portion" (Vysotskaya et al., 2021). The problem-solving in the classroom was organized in such a way that children worked in pairs with each child initially responsible for one of the quantities but then coordinating the work with the other and solving the problem using the compound unit. Children were encouraged to model the changes in quantities by drawing the images of the objects, with each student responsible for drawing objects of one kind. The children's drawings varied from realistic likenesses of the objects to symbols or even numbers of objects in a portion. The teacher did not insist on any particular type of representation but always reminded children about compound unit-based counting.

The proportionality teaching reported by Vysotskaya et al. (2021) was constructed in a form of action research, with participating teachers developing and implementing the intervention program. The intervention took twenty-six lessons of forty-five minutes each. Three months after the end of the intervention children were interviewed after solving proportionality problems, including one that was not like those practiced during the intervention.

Here are two of the problems practiced during the intervention (Vysotskaya et al., 2021, p. 438):

> Task 1. Nick is preparing presents for his friends: in each bag, he puts 2 nuts and 3 sweets. He has 18 nuts and 18 sweets. How many presents can he make?
>
> Task 2. Nick is preparing presents for his friends: in each bag, he puts 2 nuts and 3 sweets. He has 16 sweets and 12 nuts. He wants to make presents using everything he has. But he has too many … If he wants to use all of them, he should buy more … (Fill in the blanks.)

In Task 1 children are led to form a "present" that always includes two nuts and three sweets which is a compound unit in this task. One child in the pair is "responsible" for nuts while the other is responsible for sweets. Children start drawing the "presents" and at a certain moment they reach the stage when they have created six presents and the child responsible for sweets declares that there are no more sweets left. The work with the compound unit prevented children from making the typical mistake of using each quantity separately and probably declaring that nine presents (2 nuts × 9) can be prepared.

Task 2 is more complicated because it not only requires operating with a compound unit of two nuts and three sweets but also using hypothetical and inferential reasoning. For example, "16 sweets and 12 nuts allow us to make 5 presents, but we will be left with 2 nuts, and 1 sweet. If we want to use these two nuts then we need to buy more sweets."

Three months after completing the intervention the research team presented the children with similar tasks and with one new task, and conducted the interviews. All of the children were able to solve tasks similar to those given during the intervention. All of them used the compound unit working together and guided the partner's actions verbally. About half of the children informed their partners regarding their intended actions before they actually performed them. For the novel problem that required a reformulation because the conditions included the "loss" of some of the quantities, 60 percent of children correctly solved the problem. All of them, even those who had not arrived at the correct numerical answer, used the compound unit and coordinated their actions.

We conclude this section by summarizing the main features of the leading activity during the elementary school period. The leading activity is defined as formal learning. Formal learning, however, does not just mean that children go to school. It means that the goal of schooling is to prepare children for becoming "universal learners" who acquire general learning skills that can be applied to any content area. The development of general learning skills is based on the activities of critical reflection and metacognition that ultimately leads children to the stage where they are capable of distinguishing what they know from what they don't know and are capable of requesting specific help from their teachers. The implementation of the leading activity approach during this developmental period takes the form of the developmental education curriculum. This curriculum focuses on conceptual learning and "big ideas" rather than just technical subject-specific skills.

Adolescents: Interpersonal Interaction as a Leading Activity

So much is written about the conflicts and challenges of adolescence that it appears almost frivolous to talk about any leading activity during this period. After all, what is adolescence if not an age period when children, who already started perceiving themselves as "almost adults," resist any attempt of being led? That is why this period is usually portrayed via a series of developments rather than any unifying activity. The developments that are most often discussed are: "sexual maturation," "development of the self-concept," "relationships with parents," and "formal operational thought." No doubt each one of these topics is important and provides a certain understanding of the psychological changes that take place during adolescence. At the same time, it doesn't seem right to decide that the model of leading activities has nothing to contribute to a better understanding of this period.

One of the main conflicts of the adolescent age is the conflict between what appears to be a predominant activity of adolescents and what actually constitutes their leading activity. Superficially it seems that formal learning should continue to be a leading activity during this period for the simple reason that adolescents spent the major part of their lives within the school walls. They also spend more hours in school than during the previous developmental period. Moreover, if the proper education in elementary school helped children to become "universal learners" one would expect these newly acquired abilities to be at the center of adolescent life in middle and high school. However, they are not! Every psychologist and educator working with adolescents would testify to the major conflict between what school expects to be the center of students' activities (i.e., formal learning) and what students see as this center. What then is the leading activity during the period of adolescence? From the point of view of the leading activity theory, this is an activity of interpersonal interaction (Karpov, 2005).

Before bringing up some research data, let us think about our everyday experiences as observers of adolescent lives. Of course, adolescents go to school, but what do they do after school or when they skip lessons? They talk! From the point of view of many parents, their adolescent children talk endlessly. Years ago, when families had one landline phone, this constituted a major tension point between parents and children. These days, when every adolescent has his or her own smartphone or two, the "occupied landline" is no longer a problem, but parents are now concerned about the adolescents' "screen time" (Weinstein and James, 2022). Why do adolescents talk so much to each other and watch each other's postings on different social media platforms? They do this because of the separate topics mentioned at the beginning of this section. Sexual maturation leads to an increased interest in the "other." Understanding the "other" is also the way of understanding oneself. So, the formation of self-concept is inseparable from the interest in the "other" and the talk about myself and "others" with the members of my group. The ability to discuss these issues more articulately is the direct result of adolescents becoming "universal learners." Formal learning armed them with thinking and language skills that are now used for posing and contemplating such philosophical questions as "what is the meaning of life?" "why don't they understand me?" or "why should I be at home by 11 pm?"

So, how does the theory of leading activities propose to resolve the apparent conflict between the schools' responsibility to continue educating adolescents and adolescents' refusal to accept formal learning as their leading activity? The tentative answer to this question is to construct such forms of interpersonal interactions between students that contribute to the school's educational goals. The positive impact of peer interaction on learning is well known (Wentzel and Watkins, 2002); the question is how to enable such interaction so it consistently promotes the educational process without triggering adolescents' resistance. One of the possible cues in this direction is provided by nonformal education. Such nonformal contexts as scouting, sports, and amateur theater all have their own goals but all of them satisfy the adolescent needs for interpersonal interaction and exploration of social and personal roles. Bringing some of these out-of-classroom models into the school is one of the ways for constructing the leading activity for adolescents. Let us explore how this goal has been approached by leading activity practitioners using students' theater as a medium (Rubtsova, 2021).

This project fell into the educationally very challenging period of the COVID-19 pandemic. High school students spent a considerable amount of time being locked up in their homes and reported the feelings of boredom, fear, and anxiety to the project organizers.

The theoretical basis of the project included the following elements:

- The project was envisioned as a process-oriented, rather than a product-oriented, activity. It does not mean that the students were not made proud of their final performance, but both organizers and students were expected to appreciate the process of production as no less important than the result.
- The project called for the total involvement of the students in all aspects of the production, from writing the script, to designing costumes, to playing the roles.
- The project was constructed in such a way that it provided students with various opportunities for experimenting, including role exchanges during the rehearsals.
- The project was made to serve as a safe place where students are encouraged to experiment, express themselves, and not be afraid of failure or a mistake.
- The project included reflection sessions during which students were encouraged to reflect upon their interactions, discuss what they did and how they were involved in the joint activity, and share their emotions from the process.

The project started with a few introductory sessions, during which the students were given information about the project and became acquainted with the organizers. During the same introductory sessions, the students were invited to participate in role-playing improvisations, storytelling, "hot-seat" actions, etc. The aim of these introductory sessions was to motivate students to take part in the project and bring together the groups, into which the classes were divided. The second stage of the project included activities aimed at helping students to express their experiences during the lockdown period. To facilitate students' work at this stage, the organizers elaborated several tasks for them, including writing narratives on behalf of the different inanimate objects that surrounded students during lockdown (smartphones, pillows, refrigerators, etc.). The students wrote short stories and poems that conveyed their personal experiences and made videos featuring the rooms and apartments where they spent time during lockdown. Later on, students were encouraged to read their stories to each other and find similarities and differences in their experiences. This stage served as a preparation for starting to write the script. Students were given some examples of playwriting from the literature and were then split into small groups, each group responsible for writing one of the scenes of the future play. Such an arrangement provided students with an opportunity to interact with a small group and then coordinate the scenes written by different small groups.

The main character of the play written by students was a Boy who was both lonely and bored during the lockdown. While reading a book for his literature class, the Boy took a pen and wrote a poem about a girl he liked. He sent the poem to one of his friends who, however, made fun of him. Frustrated and angry by such a response, the Boy tore apart his poem and sat down on the floor. At this moment the figures of emotions and feelings (Anger, Anxiety, and Disgust) surrounded him and start arguing about what the Boy should do. The Boy fell asleep and dreamed that the famous Russian poet Alexander Pushkin came into his room and encouraged him to continue writing poems, no matter what others may think of them. The Boy then woke up and posted his poem on Facebook. At the end of the play, the Objects from the Boy's room told their own stories of living through the pandemic.

For the actual production of the play, one subgroup of students was assigned the role of actors, the second one was responsible for the design of costumes and scenery, and the third one managed the the multimedia and digital effects. Each group was offered a series of workshops on acting, scenic speech, stage movement, digital media, etc. Students "moved" between groups, provided feedback on the activities of the other groups, and coordinated group efforts to make the performance a coherent piece. When the scenes were ready, rehearsed, and video recorded students were asked to reflect upon their and their peers' work and discuss the associated feelings and emotions. By the end of the school year, the play was performed to an audience of teachers and students from other classes. From the point of view of the organizers, the main outcome of the project was the improvement of the motivation of the students, enhancement of their emotional intelligence, and alleviation of their anxiety and fears associated with the pandemic. The perspective of students is captured in the following passage written in one of the students' reflective diaries (Rubtsova, 2021, p. 111): "It was a fantastic experience. I've discovered that I'm surrounded by very interesting people. Now I know that my classmates have many talents; it's really great to study together."

It is quite appropriate that students saw the project primarily as an opportunity for interpersonal activity. We, however, can discern how the construction of such joint activities as script writing and play production contributed to the meaningful learning process. What first appeared as students' inner psychological experiences of boredom, anxiety, and fear gradually acquired the external cultural forms of the play's characters (Anger, Anxiety, and Disgust). Such a transformation says a lot about the students' abilities to grasp the essence of such a literary genre as drama which usually does not play a major role in the school curriculum. As a part of the preparation for staging the play, students participated in several workshops on writing short stories and poems on feelings and emotions. One may guess that similar assignments given as a part of regular class-room learning would be met with less enthusiasm.

So, we can analyze the following activities and their interpretations as ends or means. For the students, the leading activity was interpersonal interaction, which took place in the context of the joint activity of play-writing and production, in which learning literary genres and techniques served as supporting elements. For the school, the main educational outcome was the increased motivation of the students and their learning of literary genres and techniques which are a part of the high school curriculum. The activity of writing and staging the play served as a means for achieving goals that are important for the school.

This is just one example of how interpersonal interaction as the leading activity of adolescents can be harnessed into promoting the learning process in middle and high school. In the next section, we pose the question of what kind of leading activity or activities can be envisaged for young adults when they leave school.

Adulthood: Work as a Leading Activity

Though in his original version of the leading activity theory Elkonin (1972) suggested that work constitutes the leading activity for young adults, this suggestion has not been followed by any substantial amount of applied research. For this reason, the goal of this section is to pose some relevant questions and advance some hypotheses rather than provide any answers regarding leading activities during adulthood. The very first question that could be posed is whether it is at all legitimate to select one type of activity as a leading one for young adults. This question of course returns us to the definition of leading activities as culturally specific. Even in societies in which an absolute majority of high school graduates make a transition from school to work, there are subgroups that continue to college or university studies or have economic means that do not require gainful employment.

Already at this early stage of our discussion, we may pose an interesting question regarding the possible leading activity during the period of higher education studies. As we proposed regarding the middle and high school period, the fact that adolescents spent the major part of their days in school does not mean that formal learning constitutes their leading activity. Similarly, we can ask ourselves if the fact that university students are involved in academic learning automatically makes this learning their leading activity. One of the possible hypotheses is that the projection of possible future careers onto their current academic studies may serve as their leading activity. In other words, it is not the current study of, let us say, molecular biology but the projection of a possible future career as a biotech researcher may act as a leading activity for a university student. In this sense, one can say that work, not as an actual vocation but as an image of future work, may indeed serve as one of the leading activities of university students.

If, however, we focus on the majority of young adults who start working after high school, then we have an even more fundamental question. The fact that these young adults are involved in a vocational activity does not automatically mean that this activity is a leading one for all of them. For example, one may argue that marriage and family life constitute the leading activity for many young adults, with work serving as one of the subordinate or supporting elements. This observation leads us to an additional question regarding people who find themselves in the same context, for example, the context of a workplace but who have different leading activities. It is not difficult to imagine that for one of them, the workplace provides an opportunity to be involved in formal learning. For such a person it is not the work and its products but the process of becoming skillful in different methods and techniques that constitutes the leading activity. For another person, the workplace is first of all an arena for developing interpersonal relations. In a sense he or she still has the leading activity similar to that of adolescents, only the setting has been changed from that of school to that of the workplace. For the third and fourth persons, work indeed constitutes the leading activity, but for one of them, the work is understood as a development of concepts and products, while for the other it is an activity for gaining more money and power. Such a coexistence of

various tacitly assumed leading activities not infrequently leads to misunderstanding and conflicts, when one of the participants perceives the
workplace situation as related to concepts and products, while another one
sees it as interpersonal.

These examples of the possible copresence of various leading activities
at the workplace have implications for the previous developmental periods
as well. During practically every period, children who find themselves in
the same context may pursue different leading activities. Sometimes this
is related to developmental delays or special needs. For example, in the
context of sociodramatic play with toy cars, some children perceive these
cars as prompts for playing the social role of a driver, while others continue
with a leading activity of the previous period when toy cars had importance as an object to be manipulated rather than a prompt. One of the
typical problems at the beginning of elementary school is a gap between
children who become engaged in formal learning and other children who
perceive school as yet another setting for playful activity. Finally, the well-
known phenomenon of "nerds" and students with light autistic features
may lead to a clash between formal learning that continues to serve as the
leading activity of the former while the rest of the class is already deep in
the activity of interpersonal relations.

As a conclusion, it seems appropriate to return to the central thesis
of the leading activities approach and to elaborate its connection to the
theory of the cultural mind. The concept of leading activities was offered
as a possible alternative to the explanation of child and adolescent development. While other developmental theories focused on a prototypical
child and those physical, cognitive, and emotional changes that take place
during different stages of his or her development, this alternative approach
focused on those sociocultural activities in which children are involved
during each of the developmental periods. It was proposed to find an
activity that plays the central role during a given period and thus leads to
children's development. The leading activities model is explicitly culture-
specific; the version presented in this chapter applies only to industrial
and post-industrial societies that have systems of formal education. The
relevant research showed how the leading activities approach can be used
for the development of educational programs that may alleviate some of
the problems that plague the contemporary school. In addition, the concept of leading activities may lead to the novel conceptualization of adult
development and an explanation of conflicts engendered by the copresence of different leading activities in the same setting, such as a workplace.

CHAPTER 4

Learning Potential

What Is Hidden in the Standard Tests?

The science of the cultural mind aspires not only to interpret specifically human forms of development, cognition, and learning but also to suggest certain techniques for evaluating human abilities. Thousands and thousands of books and articles have been written about human cognition and learning. Some of them insist that these abilities are mainly innate, while others focus more on the lifelong acquisition of various cognitive and learning skills, but both the former and the latter have a tendency to look at cognition and learning almost exclusively through the prism of its products. The reason for relying on school exams, for example, is based on the assumption that the results of these exams reveal students' learning abilities. What we see in the exam results, however, is only the product rather than the process of learning. One student can achieve good exam results by investing much more time in learning the material than another student who achieved the same result but with a smaller investment of time and energy. The learning efficiency of the first is thus lower than that of the second. Can we then say, based on the exam results, that the learning ability is the same in both students? Apparently not, but this factor is hidden in a typical school exam. Moreover, what is also hidden is the very process by which these two students achieved their good exam results.

The problem of product-oriented assessment is not limited to school or college exams. In a sense, the situation is even more complicated in the case of so-called intelligence tests. During these tests, children and adults are confronted with a series of verbal, graphic, or numerical tasks that they should solve independently, usually under some time constraint. The results of the tests are interpreted as reflecting individual intellectual ability. Some psychologists claim that a well-designed intelligence test allows us to reveal the examinee's innate abilities unrelated to his or her learning experiences. Others define intelligence itself as a "general learning ability"

and suggest that intelligence tests provide us with a pretty accurate estimate of not only a person's knowledge and skills but also their learning
ability. The latter claim serves as a justification for using intelligence tests
for placing children into various educational streams. It is assumed that
the child who performed poorly on an intelligence test would not be able
to succeed in a more challenging learning environment.

The use of intelligence tests for educational placement has been chal-
lenged on many occasions. Quite legitimately, the critique focused on the
presence of culturally biased knowledge items in the intelligence tests and
on the sensitivity of the test results to the quality of education received by
students. There is, however, yet another aspect that appears to be more
important. Proper educational placement is not a mechanical act of sorting
children into subgroups with each subgroup then receiving a pre-existing
educational "package." The placement should always be accompanied by
an educational plan that takes into account not only what children know
and can do but also how they learn. This "how" is missing in the standard
intelligence tests. Somewhat akin to school exams, they show us only the
product – the number of correctly answered test questions – but we still
do not know why children failed to answer the question and what would
help them to answer it correctly. This is how this problem was highlighted
by Erika Haeussermann (1958, p. 16):

> Use of a standard test determines which of the tasks expected of the major-
> ity of children of a given age can be performed and comprehended by a
> certain child. But it does not reveal how the child has arrived at the solution
> nor whether he has had to detour impaired areas of functioning in order
> to respond appropriately to the posed task. Neither does a standard test
> explore the basis for failure when a task is failed. Yet, in order to plan an
> effective educational program for an individual child, it is as important to
> understand the pattern of his learning as it is to know the intelligence level
> or the mental age he has arrived.

Learning-Based Assessment

One of the first attempts to make the assessment process more transparent, so that not only its products but also the learning process itself
becomes transparent, was made in the 1930s. This attempt was associated with Vygotsky's (1935/2011) attempt at an understanding of what he
perceived as a "developmental paradox." What he saw as paradoxical was
the gap between the acknowledged fact that child development constitutes a dramatically rapid process, with new abilities and skills emerging

literally overnight, and the practice of assessment that focused exclusively on those abilities and skills that children could demonstrate at a given moment under conditions of independent problem-solving. Vygotsky argued that it is implausible that the child possesses only fully formed abilities and skills that are displayed during the assessment, while all others, which may emerge in a few months' time, do not exist at all. It is more reasonable to assume that there are many abilities and skills that are not completely formed but already exist in their immature form in the child's developmental "pipeline." It is these immature abilities that are crucially important for our understanding of children's development and learning because they will determine the children's performance in the near future. These abilities and skills belong to what Vygotsky called the child's Zone of Proximal Development (ZPD) (see Chaiklin, 2003).

The second paradox mentioned by Vygotsky is a gap between the typical situation of children's learning, particularly at an early age, and the situation of assessment and testing. As we mentioned in Chapter 1, adult mediation of children's learning is a norm in human society. From the earliest age, children's interaction with their environment is constantly mediated by their parents and other mentors. Joint activity with adults who help children to solve more and more challenging problems is the natural form of learning. Yet when it comes to assessment the children are left alone, and without any help or mediation they are expected to perform purely independently while being confronted with tasks that they probably see for the first time.

To resolve these paradoxes Vygotsky proposed including learning assistance provided by adults in the assessment process. So instead of giving a test or exam for an independent solution, children may first solve problems independently and then with assistance. In this way, instead of one test or exam score, children receive two: the first reflecting their existing knowledge and skills, the second reflecting their learning ability.

This is how Vygotsky (1935/2011, pp. 203–204) described his approach:

> Let us take the simplest case from our studies that can serve as a prototype of the entire problem. I studied two children when they entered school. Both were 10 years old, and both had a mental age of 8. Can I say that they are intellectually equal? Certainly! What does this mean? This means that they are capable of solving problems that correspond to the norm of 8-year-old children. Once this study is over, one can imagine that the future mental development of these children during their school years will be the same because it depends on their intelligence. Of course, it may depend on some other factors. For example, one child might be sick for half a year

while the second one attends school all the time without interruption. But apart from such cases, the future of these children is expected to be similar. Now let us imagine that instead of stopping my study when I obtain the above result, I start it again. Both children prove to be of a mental age of 8 because they are capable of solving tasks attuned to 8-year-olds but cannot solve more complex tasks. I would then demonstrate to them different methods of problem-solving. Different researchers and authors use different methods of demonstration. Some demonstrate a complete problem-solving process and then ask the child to repeat it, or start the solution and then ask the child to continue, or ask leading questions. In a word, in different ways, you prompt the child to solve the problem with your help. Under such conditions, it turns out that the first child is capable of solving tasks up to the level typical of a 12-year-old, while the second child up to the level of a 9-year-old. Can one say after this additional investigation that these children are intellectually equal?

As can be seen, Vygotsky proposed different intervention "techniques," including modeling, starting the task, and providing hints. For a better understanding of the later developments in the field of LP assessment, it is important to remember that Vygotsky merely mentioned these possible techniques but never produced anything approaching a ZPD assessment manual. His contribution, thus, was conceptual rather than technical. In which way, then, does Vygotsky's proposal change the assessment paradigm?

First of all, Vygotsky included a more "natural" form of problem-solving, which is a joint activity with an adult, into the assessment procedure. This shift corresponds to the very basis of Vygotsky's theory: his belief in the social and cultural nature of human behavior and cognition. At the same time, Vygotsky did not neglect those abilities that are already fully mastered by children and can be displayed by them independently: The goal of the first stage of the test is to identify these abilities. However, the second (i.e. interactive) phase brings two additional sources of information: information about children's ability to learn from adult's modeling, hints, and cues; and the children's ability to display, under conditions of joint activity, the emerging cognitive functions situated in the "pipeline" of their ZPD.

Learning Potential Assessment Formats

Let us now "jump" from Vygotsky's ideas about ZPD and LP formulated in the 1930s to the more recent discussions of how to implement these ideas. There are various possibilities to include the learning phase into the assessment procedure; two of the most popular were named by Sternberg and Grigorenko (2002) as the "sandwich" and "cake" formats.

The "sandwich" format presupposes three main phases: the pre-test, the learning phase, and the post-test. This format can be used both individually, with one student, and with a group. The pre-test resembles standard testing: students receive the entire test or exam and solve the problems independently. After this first phase, the assessor examines the results, identifies the most typical mistakes, and prepares the learning phase. Later on, we discuss the degree of interactivity during the learning phase allowed in different LP formats. At this moment, what is important is that the learning phase includes an active intervention of the assessor, who identifies and discusses typical mistakes, suggests more efficient problem-solving strategies, and, in more flexible formats, poses questions to the students and responds to their answers. After the learning phase, the post-test is given which is either identical to the pre-test or constitutes a parallel test of the same content and difficulty as a pre-test. The main advantage of the "sandwich" format is that it can be given to a group of students, but here also lies its limitations. While the experienced assessor is capable of identifying typical mistakes and preparing an effective learning intervention that corresponds to the needs of the students as a group, it is still possible that some students would benefit less than others from such a group-oriented intervention.

There are different ways in which one can operationalize the students' LP. The simplest way is to assume that students reveal their true potential at the post-test, irrespective of their starting point, and so the post-test score can be considered as reflecting their LP. The higher students' post-test score, the stronger is their LP. Feuerstein and his colleagues, however, strongly argued in favor of paying more attention to the gain score (the difference between post- and pre-test scores) rather than pre- or post-test scores themselves (Feuerstein et al., 1979). The gain score shows how effectively students used the learning phase for the improvement of their performance and in this way reflects their LP.

However, there is also a certain problem with using a simple gain score. In the majority of cognitive tests, items go from simple to more complex, so students who on the pre-test correctly solved the first half of the test (scored 50 out of 100) actually solved only simple and medium-level items. If at the post-test (i.e. after the learning phase) their score was 75, then the gain score is 25. Now let's consider a different subgroup of students who on the pre-test correctly solved 70 percent of the items and on the post-test 95 percent. Their gain score is the "same" – 25 – but these 25 were not the same, because they belonged to the most difficult items in the test.

To avoid the problem of the initial performance level and the difficulty of test items the method of "relative gain" was introduced. The relative gain takes into account not only the actual gain but also a "possible gain." So, students who on the pre-test received a score of 50 can gain an additional 50 points on the post-test; if, however, they actually gained only 25 points (the post-test score being 75) then the relative gain is calculated as actual gain divided by possible gain: $25/50 = 0.5$. Now let us do the same calculation for the second subgroup of students who started with a score of 70, whose gain was 25 and whose post-test score was 95. Their possible gain was $100 - 70 = 30$, while their actual gain was 25, so the relative gain is $25/30 = 0.83$ – much higher than that of the first group of students. (For these and other methods of calculating the LP scores see Budoff, 1987; Kozulin and Garb, 2004; Sergi et al., 2005).

Group Learning Potential Assessment

Now let us examine how the "sandwich" format of LP assessment has been practically used and for which purposes. As already mentioned, one of the advantages of this format is that it can be implemented not only individually but also for groups of students. This advantage has been fully used by Feuerstein and his colleagues who faced the task of identifying the LP of a rather large number of new immigrant adolescents from Ethiopia in Israel (see Kaniel et al., 1991). New immigrant adolescents arrived in Israel one year prior to the study and were placed in boarding schools sponsored by the Youth Aliyah Department of the Jewish Agency. The majority of youngsters came from rural areas of Ethiopia and had very limited school experience if any. The boarding schools' administration reported the low level of performance of the new immigrants and questioned their intellectual level. The goal of Feuerstein and his colleagues was to investigate if there is a significant difference between the performance of immigrant youth on such standard intelligence tests as Raven's Standard Progressive Matrices (RSPM) (Raven, 1958) on the one hand and their LP on the other. Feuerstein insisted that LP is much more important for educational planning than the absolute level of standardized test performance of immigrant youth.

Three hundred new immigrant adolescents were examined using the group version of the "sandwich" LP test (Kaniel et al., 1991). The pre- and post-tests were performed in a standard fashion using such a nonverbal and presumably culturally neutral test as RSPM without time limitation. The learning phase included active mediation provided by the assessors who presented students with a series of matrix tasks (Set Variations 2) specially designed by Feuerstein's teams (Feuerstein et al., 1979). The Set

Variations tasks are based on selected items of the RSPM that are systematically varied and modified in terms of their content and complexity so that a full range of problem-solving strategies can be learned with the help of these tasks. There were five series of the Set Variations tasks; each series started with a model task that was mediated to the students by the assessor. After mediation was over, the students practiced problem-solving using the remaining items in the given series of the Set Variations. After that, the mediation of the model task of the next series was given, and so on to the end of all series of the Set Variations.

Mediation was based on Feuerstein's criteria of mediated learning (discussed in Chapter 1). The assessor actively engaged students by drawing their attention to the task ("What do you think we should do here?"), analyzing different possible answers ("Why do you think that No. 5 is a correct answer? What is wrong with the answer No 2?"), discussing strategies ("We first compare three designs in the upper row, then three designs in the middle row, and finally the two designs in the third row in which the third design is missing"), and expanding and generalizing ("Though these tasks look different they are based on the same principle. What is this principle? Right, all of them are based on the principle of analogy").

The initial level of the students' performance on RSPM was much lower than that of the Israeli norm for their age. On average, new 15-year-old immigrant students performed at the level of 10-year-old native Israelis. If this static measure of the new immigrant students' intelligence were the only one taken into the account, many of them would have to be placed in special education classes. Fortunately, the LP procedure offers a different perspective. By introducing a learning phase based on the material of Set Variations, the evaluation was transformed from static to dynamic. The gain scores were calculated and the performance of students who received mediation was compared to the control group consisting of their peers who received the same tasks but without mediation. The first important finding was that mere familiarity with the test material does not help much in solving the tasks. The control group of fifty-seven students who solved the RSPM test twice improved their performance only by 3 percent. So, it is mediated learning rather than repeated exposure to the material that leads to the improvement of problem-solving. The second finding was that on average the post-test results of immigrant students were much closer to the Israeli age norm. So, with proper mediation, at least some immigrant students were able to solve the same RSPM tasks as native Israelis. Finally, the comparison of the pre-and post-test scores indicated that the average simple gain score of the immigrant students was a rather impressive 23 percent. Using the more modern effect size measure (Cohen's *d*) the pre-to post-test gain was *d* = 1.16 – a pretty large effect size.

These studies were the first in the series of LP projects conducted by Feuerstein and his team with new immigrants from Ethiopia. The results of these studies consistently demonstrated a rather large gap between immigrants' standard test performance and their LP. The gap was observed not only among the low-functioning immigrant students but also among their more successful immigrant peers. For the latter group, the LP assessment opened the gates to more prestigious university programs. The standard psychometric scores of immigrant students were sufficient for admission only to less prestigious tracks. The university administration agreed to implement an alternative admission procedure based on LP assessment rather than standard psychometric scores. Using the LP group assessment similar to the one described above, but with more challenging tasks (graphic, numerical, and verbal), it was possible to identify candidates with higher LP. The follow-up study confirmed that the selected immigrant students successfully completed their BA studies and that their drop-out rate was lower than that of nonimmigrant students (Feuerstein et al., 2019). We can conclude this section by stating that group LP assessments using the "sandwich" format achieved at least one of the important assessment goals: They provided significant additional information about the LP of immigrant students and in this way opened for them educational opportunities that would be denied to them if only standard tests and exams were used.

The Range of Learning Potential

Historically the LP approach focused predominantly on socially disadvantaged, immigrant, and special needs children. Thus, one of the primary goals of LP assessment was to create situations in which underachieving students can learn the prerequisite skills and demonstrate their ability to apply these skills in problem-solving. At the same time, it was tacitly assumed that students with normative development do not have a major gap between their learning potential and standard test performance, and therefore for them LP assessment is not of crucial importance. For the students with atypical development or a nonstandard educational history, on the other hand, LP turned out to be a much better predictor of their future educational performance than static scores. These findings supported the image of LP as a technique for revealing the "hidden" potential of special needs students (Guthke et al., 1995).

The question of LP versus current performance may, however, be posed in a broader context that reaches beyond the goal of revealing the hidden abilities of low-performing students. If one accepts that problem-solving on the one hand and learning on the other constitute two different forms of human intellectual activity, then all individuals irrespective of their level of functioning are expected to show some difference between their ability to solve problems and their ability to benefit from learning situations.

Methodologically it is not easy to check this hypothesis, because it requires identifying a sufficient number of subjects with the same cognitive performance score established with the help of static tests and then evaluating their LP. Such an opportunity became available in the process of conducting the vocational assessments of 500 young adults (Kozulin, 2010). The assessment was commissioned by a governmental organization responsible for the promotion of employment among young adults from lower-SES families. The project participants (age range 18–29) had completed twelve years of schooling and had no documented special educational needs. The goal of the assessment was to select candidates for various vocational training programs that required different levels of learning and problem-solving skills. All participants were pre-tested using a standard, static RSPM test. This allowed the identification of reasonably large subgroups of subjects who had practically the same RSPM scores (with a difference of one to two points). After the static RSPM test, all subjects were given Set Variations in LP format, that is, with the first (model) task in each series mediated to the participants by the assessor followed by the subjects' solution of the remaining tasks in this series. Mediation involved analysis of the model task, direct teaching of problem-solving principles, probing questions, and eliciting responses from the participants.

The Set Variation scores were calculated for the thirty-three participants who had the same RSPM scores, and the participants were divided into high-LP and low-LP subgroups based on a median split. The difference between the Set Variations scores of these two subgroups was very large: 2.2 SD (standard deviation) (Kozulin, 2010). If we assume that Set Variations scores provide us with the estimation of the participants' LP, while the RSPM scores provide their pre-existing problem-solving skills, these results confirm that people who have the same level of problem-solving skills may have a very different LP (see Figure 4.1). One may thus conclude that LP assessments are important not only for underachieving and special needs students but also for a wider range of populations. This is because the LP paradigm demonstrates that successful problem-solving on the one hand and efficient learning on the other, though connected, are not identical.

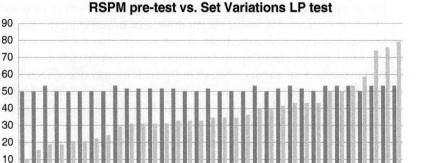

Figure 4.1 Results of static matrices test vs. LP test

Graduated Prompts

As already mentioned, the "sandwich" format can be used also for individual LP assessments. A student is first given a complete test then the assessor analyzes the student's mistakes, prepares the learning phase, and engages the student in an interactive "lesson" followed by the post-test. There is, however, a different format that might be more suitable for individual LP assessments. Sternberg and Grigorenko (2002) named it the "cake" format. As the layer cake has several different layers, this form of LP assessment presupposes that a student's response to each test item is followed by a short learning phase, often in the form of feedback or a hint given by the assessor. One of the more popular types of the "cake" format is the so-called graduated prompts procedure (see Budoff, 1987; Ferrara et al., 1986).

Students are given the first in a series of tasks, and if their response is correct then the second task is given, and so on. The moment the response is incorrect, the first hint is given, after which the task is given again. If the first hint proves to be ineffective, the second hint is given, and so on until the final hint provides the student with the solution to the problem. This procedure doesn't leave students without the correct solutions to the tasks. The LP is operationalized as the opposite of the number of received hints: The LP is lower in those students who received more hints and higher in those who required less.

To get a better idea of how this approach works, let us consider the following letter sequence completion task:

L Z T B M Z U B __ __ __ __ __ __ __ __

There are two main forms of prompting: linear prompts and hierarchical prompts. The linear prompting always adds the same amount of information with each hint. In this task, the first hint is to fill the first blank with a correct letter, the second hint is to fill the second blank with a correct letter, and so on:

First hint: L Z T B M Z U B **N** __ __ __ __ __ __ __
Second hint: L Z T B M Z U B **N Z** __ __ __ __ __ __

The hierarchical prompts are based on a different principle. The initial hints are of a more general nature and aim at focusing students' attention and providing them with a general orientation in the task. Subsequent hints become more and more specific until they provide students with an exact algorithm for solving the problem.

The sequence of hierarchical hints in the letter completion task might take the following form:

Hint 1. "Look at the task again. Do you understand what should be done?"

Hint 2. "Are any of the letters written more than once in the task? … Which ones? … Does this give you any idea how to continue the pattern?"

Hint 3. "Do any of the letters in this task appear next to each other in the alphabet? Does this help you to solve the problem?"

Hint 4. "How many other letters are there between the L and the M in the task? … And how many other letters are there between the T and the U? … Does this give you any ideas about the solution ?"

Hint 5. "There are three letters between L and M and three letters between M and the first blank. If we were going to continue this pattern, what letter do you think we should put in the blank?"

Hint 6. "There are always three other letters between Z and the next Z and three other letters between B and the next B. Put Zs and Bs into their places."

Hint 7. "M appears three letters after L because it is next to the L in the alphabet. N will appear three letters after M because it is next to the M in the alphabet, and O because it is next to N. The same about T _ _ _U_ _ _V _ _ _W. Complete the task."

Students' LP is operationalized as the opposite of the number of hints required for the solution; however, the "weight" of each one of the hierarchical hints is different. For example, students who needed only the first hint can be described as having a good level of independent problem-solving – they benefited from focusing their attention but did not need specific problem-solving strategies. Students who needed the first three hints were unable to find the strategy themselves, but once it was given to them in a general way ("letters written more than once" and "letters that appear next to each other in the alphabet") they were able to apply it to a concrete problem. The type of learning required for students who required hints four, five, or six is of a much more concrete level and thus their LP is lower than that of the others.

Of course, the actual LP assessment based on graduated prompts has more than one task. In this example, two types of relationships – "identity" (repetition of the same letter) and "next" (the appearance of letters in alphabetical order) – and the periodicity of the letters were used. The complete test may start with simpler relationships such as "identity–identity–next–next" and gradually come to more complex tasks: those that involve not only alphabetically next but also alphabetically previous. By comparing the dynamics of students' need for hints in increasingly more complex tasks we can identify different learning profiles. One such profile is linear: the more difficult the task, the more hints students need. Some students, however, proved to be quick learners as long as the task was of the same type (e.g. "identity–identity–next–next"), but required more hints when the task has been changed to, for example, "identity–next–identity–next." Later all we return to the question of the relationship between LP and the generalizability of learned strategies.

Learning Potential Assessment: Scripted or Flexible?

One of the issues that has remained a focus of LP discussions since the 1960s was the degree of standardization of the learning phase of LP assessment. As we saw in the example with the letter sequence task, it is rather easy to design a liner prompts procedure that is highly standardized: Each time the wrong answer is given, a standard hint (one of the correct letters) is given. The hierarchical prompts can also be standardized, though here there might be a wide difference in opinion regarding the most appropriate formulation of the hint at each one of the prompting levels. The obvious advantage of using the standardized sequence of hints is the ability to compare the LP performance of different students and to conduct systematic research. At the same time, an obvious disadvantage of standardization is the lack of sensitivity of this procedure to the particular learning needs of a given student. The work of Budoff (1987) and Ferrara et al. (1986) represent an LP assessment suitable for standardization, while the work of Feuerstein, et al. (1979) demonstrated the advantages of more flexible mediation.

We use the letter sequence task to demonstrate how the same task might be presented in a rigidly scripted vs. flexibly mediated form. The scripted assessment starts with the presentation of the task to a student. If the student gives a wrong answer (wrong continuation of the sequence) or no answer, then the assessor provides the first hint: "Look at the task again. Do you understand what should be done?" exactly in these words. In the flexible meditational LP assessment, some form of mediation can be provided, however, even before the student makes a mistake. More or less the same words are used – "Look at the task. What do you think should be done here?" – but these words do not play the role of a scripted hint, instead serving as the starting point of a meditational dialogue between the assessor and the student. Depending on the student's responses the assessor may draw their attention to "what is present" (sequence of letters) and "what is missing" (something in the blank spaces). Only after such a preliminary mediation that orients students in the task does the first student's own attempt at problem-solving take place. The assessor's response to the student's mistakes is also more flexible. For example, if the student responds by just copying the already existing sequences (L Z T B M Z U B *L Z T B M Z U B*), instead of the standard hint "Are any of the letters written more than once in the task?" – which is not relevant in this case – the mediator draws the student's attention to the difference between "continuing the pattern" and "copying the pattern." A flexible assessment based on Feuerstein's criteria of mediated learning also requires the inclusion of generalization and transfer into the assessment procedure. The assessor leads students to the general formulation of the principles of "identity" (the same letter) and "next" (next in alphabetical order) and then asks them to construct a similar task but with digits instead of letters. In this way, the flexible mediation procedure is capable of accumulating richer information about each individual learner. This richness, however, comes at the expense of efficiency because it requires more time and almost prevents the comparison of the performance of different students because the mediation received by each one of them is different.

Researchers and practitioners working in the field of LP continue searching for an optimal combination of scripted sequences of prompts with some degree of meditational freedom. One of the recent attempts of this type was made by Hasson (2018) in designing her dynamic assessment of sentence structure (DASS). The goal of DASS was to create a procedure that would generate LP-relevant information and help to develop more precise intervention strategies for children who have already been diagnosed as having language disorders. So, DASS is not a diagnostic procedure but a procedure aimed at identifying the LP profile of the target group of children.

The DASS material includes sentence anagrams with words printed on a single card in random order, for example: "SINGING AND IS MOTHER FATHER DRIVING IS." Children are asked to formulate two sentences from the given words. As long as children accurately formulate the sentences they are allowed to work independently; hierarchical prompts are provided only when children experience difficulties with one of the items. The prompting procedure includes five levels – from general metacognitive orientation to very specific help with a given item. So, on the one hand, we have here a classical graduated prompts sequence – from general to more concrete. At the same time, Hasson (2018, p. 62) was very specific in stating that: "The actual cues are not prescribed or scripted, but may be expressed, and are mediated, in a flexible and individualized way, depending on the needs of the child and his responses during the test."

At Level 1 there is no prompting as such, but an introductory question: "Do you know what you have to do?" If children solve the task correctly without responding to the question, they nevertheless score the point and can move to the second item. Mediation at Level 2 helps children to refocus their attention to the task if they become distracted. On the same level is assistance with some words that might be unfamiliar to children. On the third level of prompting, children who failed to respond to more general attention focusing cues (Level 2) are provided with help in forming strategies and problem-solving methods. At this level, in counter-distinction to the more concrete fourth and fifth levels, strategies are still general and potentially transferable to other materials. The assessors are given considerable freedom in choosing how to provide mediation to children. They may ask "which one you can start with?" or "can you make little groups of words?," or a more concrete hint, "can you swap the words around?" Each one of these strategies can actually be applied to every one of the sentences in the DASS test. The assessor thus can evaluate to what extent mediation at the third level is capable of promoting children's strategies in application not only to a given item but to the following items as well.

The entire DASS procedure is infused with Feuerstein's criteria of mediated learning (see Chapter 1), primarily intentionality and reciprocity (focusing children's attention and being sensitive to their responses), mediation of meaning (explaining the reasons for various actions and their importance), mediation of feeling of competence (praise and encouragement), regulation of behavior (reducing impulsiveness and guessing), and transcendence of acquired strategies and skills to the new material. By combining the flexibility in formulating prompts at each one of the levels with maintaining the set sequence of levels and the corresponding scoring procedure, Hasson aimed at creating a procedure that may benefit from both a set structure and the degrees of meditational freedom.

Learning Potential and Cognitive Modifiability

One of the ways, if not to resolve but at least to reformulate the issue of the scripted vs. flexible mediated procedures, is to distinguish between dynamic (or LP) assessment and dynamic (or LP) testing. Sternberg and Grigorenko (2002, p. 30) argued: "Broadly defined, dynamic assessment is naturally linked with intervention. In essence, the goal of dynamic assessment is to intervene and to change. The goal of dynamic testing, however, is much more modest – it is to see whether and how the participant will change if an opportunity is provided." In a somewhat broader theoretical context, the same issue can be tackled by comparing the concept of cognitive modifiability and the concept of LP. When the assessment or testing is viewed through the lens of LP, especially in its scripted form, the goal appears to be the evaluation of the student's ability to benefit from models, hints, and examples during the performance of the learning tasks. As discussed earlier, LP defined in this way can be operationalized as a minimal number of hints required for solving given tasks and may help to predict students' performance in future learning situations. For example, as demonstrated by Sternberg and Grigorenko (2002), the efficiency of learning the rules of an artificial language through a series of samples may serve as an indicator of the student's potential for learning foreign languages.

On the other hand, the assessment of cognitive modifiability appears to focus on the ability of children to change radically their type of performance and their readiness for the transition from one cognitive-developmental stage to the next one. Thus, Feuerstein et al. (1979, p. 91) explicitly set up such radical modifiability as one of the major goals of their assessment: "[T]he extent of examinee's modifiability in terms of levels of functioning made accessible to him by the process of modification, and the significance of the levels attained by him in the hierarchy of cognitive functions."

There is, however, a very serious terminological confusion when it comes to the use of such terms as LP assessment, dynamic assessment, dynamic testing, and the assessment of cognitive modifiability. Even Feuerstein, who seemed to state quite clearly his interest in cognitive modifiability, named his assessment battery the "Learning Potential Assessment Device" (Feuerstein et al., 1979). Terminological inconsistency has not remained unnoticed by critics, who pointed to the vagueness of many of the formulations employed by the LP assessment practitioners (see Hessels-Schlatter and Hessels, 2009; Karpov and Tzuriel, 2009). It thus seems appropriate to identify the restructuring of a wide range of cognitive functions as a sign of cognitive modifiability, while the efficiency of using such devices as models, prompts, and cues for the solution of a more restricted range of tasks as indicative of students' LP. One might then be able to distinguish between students with good LP but relatively low modifiability, and those with slower learning but greater modifiability potential.

In a series of studies using the graduated prompts, Brown and Ferrara (1985) were able to distinguish between the students' cognitive ability as reflected in their IQ scores, their LP operationalized through the number of standardized hints needed for reaching the criterion, and the ability to generalize and transfer strategies learned during the LP test to the new tasks. Students with "average IQ" (mean 101) and "high IQ" (mean 122) participated in the study. If the problem-solving ability reflected in the IQ scores were indistinguishable from the learning ability, then all "high-IQ" students would have been "fast learners," and all "average IQ" students "slow learners." The results, however, demonstrated that for about 30 percent of the students their LP could not be predicted by their IQ scores. Though the majority of "high-IQ" students indeed turned out to be "fast learners," some of them demonstrated slow learning, while some of the "fast learners" had a lower IQ. For the current discussion, it is even more important that only some of the "fast learners" proved to be good "transferrers" to the new and more distant tasks. Learning from hints and applying the learned strategies to similar material may indeed reflect the students' LP, while their ability to generalize the strategies and with their help change the level of their problem-solving activity apparently belongs to cognitive modifiability.

The results similar to those of Brown and Ferrara (1985) were obtained by Kozulin (2011) in his study of primary school immigrant children in which some of Feuerstein's LP tasks were used. Students' performance in the LP test that used a mediated model task followed by the sequence of similar tasks for independent problem-solving was contrasted with the students' ability to apply the thus learned strategies to a wider range of Raven Matrices tasks. The results of the study demonstrated that about 27 percent of children fall within the so-called mixed groups by showing good LP in the LP test but low modifiability or good modifiability but relatively low LP.

The Facet Design of Learning Potential Assessments

The exploration of the issue of the possible difference between LP and cognitive modifiability prompted us to return to the initial proposals for LP assessments formulated by Feuerstein. As we will see, not all of these early proposals had been implemented in his later work. The initial proposal of Feuerstein (1968b, p. 9) for LP assessment included the following principles:

> First, to measure the capacity of the examinee to acquire a given principle, learning set, skill, and attitude; second, to measure the child's capacity to apply these acquisitions with respect to a variety of tasks progressively removed from the initial one on which the acquisition was induced; third, the amount of teaching investment required in order to modify the level of functioning of the individual as compared with his initial level of functioning; forth, transferability – the significance of attaining modification in the development of adequate reaction patterns in areas of behavior other than those actually modified.

To implement these principles into the form of an LP assessment battery, Feuerstein proposed to use Guttman's (1959) facet design. After analyzing several intelligence tests, Guttman came up with the idea of presenting the assessment material and situation as a series of "facets." Facet A focuses on the test items and specifies that they can be present, for example in verbal, numerical, and geometric modalities. Facet B focuses on the examinee's performance and specifies that this performance can be, for example, oral, paper and pencil, or manual manipulation. Facet C specifies the required operations, for example inference from the rule, application of the rule, or learning the rule. Facet D presents the range of the examinee's responses to test items. The assessment as a whole, including materials, procedures, and responses, can thus be imagined as a series of "facets."

Using Guttman's idea of the facet design, Feuerstein (1968a) offered a model of the Learning Potential Assessment Device (LPAD) that included an initial cognitive principle and then a series of tasks progressively more and more distant from the initial example (see Figure 4.2). He also suggested that the same cognitive principle should be realized in the tasks presented in different modalities: verbal-logical, geometric, pictorial, and numerical.

If one compares this initial proposal to the LPAD battery actually developed by Feuerstein et al. (1979), one can immediately see that the entire potential of the initial facet design had not been realized. Feuerstein's actual LPAD battery included some tests (e.g. Set Variations

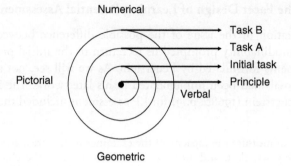

Figure 4.2   Initial model of LPAD (based on Feuerstein, 1968a)

of Raven Matrices) which included items progressively more distant from the initial ones, but retained the same modality (geometric) and did not specify the criteria of transferability. Some tests in this battery, such as a sixteen-word memory test, had neither different modalities nor progressively more complex or distant items. Only one test – Tri-modal Analogy, had the variation of the presentation modality (pictorial–geometric–verbal) and variation of different types of analogies (e.g. part–whole, or cause–effect).

One may of course argue that Feuerstein's LPAD battery as a whole had a sufficient variation of the complexity of the tasks and their modalities. However, in the absence of the systematic application of the facet design, the tests remained separated from each other. As a result, one of the more challenging elements of Feuerstein's assessment model became the task of combining the results obtained in various tests into an integrative LP report. One may assume that the challenge of integration stems from the fact that the facet design of the battery as a whole was somehow "lost" in the process of the actual development of specific LPAD tasks.

In what follows, we outline the hypothetical design of the LP test that would correspond to the original proposal based on the facet model:

Cognitive principle. Let us assume that the cognitive principle that forms the center of our test is: "the same parts can form different wholes."

Initial mediation. The principle is explained to students using a model pictorial task, for example how the same elements (doors, windows) create different images of the house.

Task 1. The same content, the same modality, greater complexity. The task uses the same content (houses), and the same modality (pictorial), but a greater number of elements (e.g. doors, windows, chimney). ("Use all given elements to create as many different houses as possible.")

Task 2. Change in the content and modality. The principle is the same ("The same parts can form different wholes"), but instead of elements of the houses in pictorial modality, geometric shapes are used. For example, three squares form different composite figures.

Task 3. Different content, same modality, greater complexity. The modality is still geometrical, but instead of three squares, four triangles are given.

Task 4. Different content and different modality. The shift from visual (pictorial or geometric) to verbal modality. For example, the assembly of different words from the same letters (e.g. ACT-CAT, ARTS-RATS-STAR-TSAR). Then the assembly of different sentences composed of the same words (e.g. SINGING AND IS MOTHER FATHER DRIVING IS) "Mother is singing, and father is driving" and "Father is singing, and mother is driving."

Task 5. Different content and different modalities. The same cognitive principle but in the tasks of numerical modality. For example, using the same digits (e.g. 1, 2, 3) for generating different numbers: 123, 132, 213, 231, 312, 321. Or analyzing the number into its constituent elements: $12 = 2 \times 6$, 3×4, $1 + 11$, $6 + 6$, etc.

According to LP methodology, for each stage of the assessment, a series of prompts is prepared and provided to the examinees if they fail to solve the problem. The number and explicitness of prompts will point to the LP of the examinees.

After completing the series of tasks based on one principle, the examinees are given the next series, based, for example, on the principle: "You need a complete set of elements to form a complex whole." In verbal modality, the examinees should select a set of words that allows for forming the target sentence. In geometric modality, the examinees should select a set of geometric elements that together create a target complex figure. In pictorial modality, the examiner should select a set of drawings that together give a target picture. In numerical modality, the examinee should select a set of numbers the sum of which gives a target number.

Adaptive Assessment

Up to this point, we discussed the issues of LP assessment and testing as they appeared in what one may call the "LP community." Starting with the pioneering work of Vygotsky, Feuerstein, and Budoff and up to the present moment, a considerable number of developments and discussions took place "inside" this community, including the issue of LP assessment formats, their degree of flexibility, relationships between LP assessment, and standard intelligence testing. During the last decade, however, it has been possible to observe some developments that took place "outside" the LP community but which may provide an interesting new perspective on the issue of learning-based assessments. The first of these "external" developments is the so-called adaptive assessment.

The initial goals of the methodology of adaptive assessment had very little in common with the concerns of the LP community. These goals focused on making standard exams in such school subjects as mathematics more efficient (see Kingsbury et al., 2014). One of the problems with standard exams is that they aim at an average student of a given grade level. As a result, weaker-than-average students find the majority of exam items too difficult, while stronger-than-average students find the exam insufficiently challenging. An exam that has a wider range of items is impractical because it requires too much time to take and more time for a teacher to check. In addition, the immediacy of learning about correct and incorrect answers is lost because it takes a considerable time for teachers to check the exams and to give the results to students.

The idea of adaptive assessment was to compensate for these shortcomings of the standard exams. The availability of computer technology helped greatly in achieving this goal. Instead of having one exam for all students, the adaptive assessment approach starts with creating a very large database of exam items, ranging from easy to more complex. The algorithm is created that defines which item is given depending on the student's response to the previous item: If the previous item was solved successfully the next item is more challenging, if the response to the previous item is incorrect the next item is the easier one. In this way, students working individually via the computer receive items that correspond to the level of performance of each one of them. The feedback (right/wrong) is given immediately and automatically.

Some studies of adaptive exams showed that they appear to be as accurate as standard paper-and-pencil tests that are twice as long. This enabled the exam to have fewer questions and to take less time while providing sufficient information about student performance. As expected, adaptive exams provide more and more accurate information about the performance of students who are struggling and students who are excelling. The availability of immediate feedback to both teachers and students created more favorable conditions for the quicker adjustment of instruction to the needs of students (Kingsbury et al., 2014).

This overview does not imply that there are no internal discussions or challenges within the adaptive assessment approach; our goal here is not to elaborate on these discussions but to show how some of the adaptive assessment trends seem to move in the direction of LP assessment. The main difference between a typical adaptive assessment that allows individualized provision of exam items and an LP-oriented adaptive assessment is that the latter includes instructional prompts. Similar to the more tightly scripted graduated prompts procedures, the LP-oriented adaptive assessment is based on an algorithm that evaluates the wrong responses given by students and provides them the relevant hints and explanations. Wang (2011) designed such an LP-oriented computerized assessment in mathematics for junior high school students. The system included main items, alternate-form items, and three levels of hints. The computer interface includes the problem (text and graphics) and four multiple-choice answers. The inclusion of alternate-form items reflecting the same concepts and operations as the main items served the purpose of checking that students indeed selected the correct answer rather than simply being lucky the first time in their choice. Level 1 hints provide an explanation of the problem and clarify conditions. Level 2 hints explained the relevant math concepts, and Level 3 hints demonstrated how to solve a similar problem with simplified numbers or provided detailed problem-solving steps for the target problem. The research conducted by Wang (2011) demonstrated that the use of LP-oriented assessment was more effective in enhancing students' mathematical problem-solving in comparison to other methods, such as standard web-based exams or paper-and-pencil exams. The hints suggested by Wang appear to be close enough to those of LP-graduated prompts not only in that they go from more general to more specific, but also that at least Level 1 prompts are more "cognitive" than narrowly mathematical.

The assessment of mathematical learning designed by Wu et al. (2017) can be used as an example of the additional advantages of using algorithms for the analysis of students' responses and providing them with relevant prompts. Wu's assessment aimed at evaluating primary school students' ability to solve the problems of addition and subtraction of fractions with different denominators. The multiple-choice answers reflected the possible misconceptions regarding fractions. The sequence of prompts thus focused on specific misconceptions demonstrated by students who selected one of the incorrect answers.

For example, let us consider the following task:

4/5 = ( )/40, what is the number in ( )?
Students were to select one of the following answers: 8, 10, 32, 39.

If students selected 8, they receive the first prompt:

Incorrect! Your answer is 40/5 = 8
What is expansion?

If at the second attempt the response is still incorrect, students receive the second prompt:

Incorrect!
The numerator is 5 × 8 = 40
How to expand the denominator?

After the third unsuccessful attempt students are given the direct instruction:

"The expansion refers to multiplying the numerator and denominator by the same (bigger than 1) integer, which results in a fraction that is equivalent to the original fraction." Multiplying the numerator and denominator of 4/5 by 8, that is, 4 × 8/5 × 8 = 32/40, so the number in ( ) is 32.

The first two prompts are of course different in the case of other incorrect answers. For example, if students selected 39 as the answer, the first prompt will be:

Incorrect!
Your answer is 39 − 1 = 40
What is expansion?

The second prompt:

Incorrect!
The expansion of a fraction is not the numerator minus the denominator. How to expand the denominator?

The third prompt, however, is the same for all incorrect answers because it contains a direct instruction on how to solve the problem.

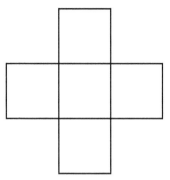

Figure 4.3   The area and perimeter task

To evaluate the effectiveness of this procedure Wu et al. (2017) compared the mathematical test performance of three groups of primary school students: All three groups received static math tests before and after the intervention. The first group's intervention took the form of an adaptive LP test with prompts described earlier, the second group received individualized instruction without adaptive prompts, and the third group received traditional classroom math instruction. The results showed that the pre- to post-test gain was higher in the adaptive LP group. This indicates that the LP assessment procedure not only provided LP information about students but also served as an important instructional strategy.

The close association between LP assessment and instruction can be gleaned in the studies conducted with the help of the "ASSISTment" system that allows not only assessing students but also providing them with relevant homework. The system started as a computerized platform for adaptive math assessment that included some cues and hints (see Feng et al., 2009). Students were first shown a task, for example, something like the one shown in Figure 4.3.

"The area of each square in the figure is 16 square units. What is the perimeter of the figure?"

If students gave wrong answers, they were provided with two scaffolding questions. First: "What is the length of one side of a square in the figure?" If students' responses to this question were unsatisfactory, they were given feedback, for example: "No, you might be thinking about the area of each square, but you are looking for the length of one side of a square" and then given a prompt: "The area of a square is equal to the product of the length of its two sides." The second scaffolding question was: "Now you have enough information to find the perimeter of the figure. What do you think it is?"

As mentioned above, originally ASSISTment had been developed as a system for individualized adaptive math assessment that in addition to evaluating the students' math performance provided teachers with information about the effectiveness of prompts and scaffolding questions in enhancing the students' mathematical learning. The next step, however, was to use this platform for providing students with individualized homework that included immediate feedback with prompts and scaffolding questions. A large-scale study was conducted in the state of Maine. The study compared the effectiveness of the homework provided by the teachers using the ASSISTment platform and teachers who used the standard homework assignments without prompts or scaffolding (Murphy et al., 2020).

In what concerns the mathematical content, teachers could assign problems from their textbook, create their own problems, or select problems from an existing set of Skill Builder problems available on the ASSISTment platform. For the problems from the textbook, students received immediate feedback (correct or incorrect), and if the solution was incorrect the students could make additional attempts and enter new solutions. The Skill Builder problems allowed for a wider range of feedback. When students experienced difficulty with a particular problem they could request and receive step-by-step hints about the solution of the problem. Students received similar problems until they answered a sequence of three problems correctly. Teachers also had an option of reassessing students automatically on particular skills one or two weeks after the successful completion of the Skill Builder problem set.

There are several results from this study (Murphy et al., 2020) that are relevant to the present discussion about the relationships between assessments and intervention. First of all, similar to some of the LP assessment studies, the homework via ASSISTment study demonstrated that students who started the year with lower mathematics scores made greater progress than students with higher beginning-of-the-year scores. This is an interesting result if one takes into account the so-called Mathew effect (Otto and Kistner, 2017) that is often observed during intervention studies when stronger students benefit more from the intervention than weaker students. So, it appears that the inclusion of the assessment elements into the intervention project made it more beneficial to initially weaker students. The second important result is the impact of the type of homework on the end-of-the-year results. Students whose teachers used more of the Skill Builder problems and fewer standard textbook problems made greater gains. The main difference between standard textbook problems and Skill Builder problems was that prompts and scaffolding questions were more elaborate in the case of the Skill Builder tasks. This further supports the thesis that the inclusion of the LP type of tasks into the homework material is more effective than simple (correct/incorrect) feedback. We will continue exploring the relationships between LP assessments and intervention in the next section dedicated to the RTI approach.

Response to Intervention

Another development that took place outside the LP mainstream but eventually influenced it was the RTI methodology (Grigorenko, 2009; Vaughn et al., 2014). Initially, RTI was introduced as an alternative procedure for identifying children with a "specific learning disability/disorder." The older and still practiced identification procedure is based on the discrepancy between children's IQ and their reading achievement. Children whose IQ scores were in the normal range but whose reading achievements were significantly lower than expected based on their IQ were considered to have specific learning disabilities or disorders and were provided with special educational services. One of the driving forces behind the development of RTI procedures was the need for more effective prevention measures that could assist "at-risk" children without labeling them as "learning disabled." The use of the discrepancy criterion resulted in a considerable number of false-positive cases in which children were identified with a specific learning disability and received special education when they could have been assisted adequately within the framework of regular education. There were also false-negative cases, namely children who showed no discrepancy but who actually needed learning support. Thus, RTI was viewed as a possible way of avoiding erroneous placement of those children who, in fact, do not need special education services and providing these services to those children who indeed need them. Thus, prevention and more effective teaching in the context of regular education are key concepts associated with RTI. Though the RTI model can be used not only with reading but also with writing or mathematics, in what follows we focus on reading because it remains the main target of RTI.

The RTI procedure starts with either the entire class or with a selected group of children who demonstrate reading difficulty. Reading intervention is given for at least ninety minutes per day. Assessments are conducted every three months throughout the school year. Those children who do not respond to this form of intervention are placed in small groups (four to five students per group) with more focused intervention for thirty minutes per day (in addition to the ninety minutes for the entire group). This additional intervention is given either by an appropriately trained classroom teacher or a reading specialist. The progress is monitored twice a month on target skills. Those children who still show no progress are given yet another additional level of intervention which includes two forty-five-minute sessions per day with a reading specialist one-on-one or in groups of two to three students. The progress is monitored twice a month. Only those students who fail to demonstrate reading progress after these three levels of intervention are recommended for special education services appropriate for children with specific learning disabilities.

One can see that RTI and LP assessment have one conceptual element in common: Children's abilities and needs are evaluated dynamically by closely monitoring children's response to a certain type of learning intervention. Taking into account that the RTI model has been developed without the direct involvement of LP assessment specialists, the commonality outlined earlier testifies to a certain paradigmatic shift that has taken place in the educational field. RTI brought a dynamic dimension to the definition of reading ability and as such has the potential for becoming a precursor of significant changes in the entire philosophy of classroom assessment.

At the same time, as has been elaborated by Grigorenko (2009) and Lidz and Pena (2009) there appear to be some significant differences between RTI and LP assessment. LP assessment of language and reading, like any other form of LP assessment, focuses mainly on the cognitive and meta-cognitive strategies and skills of the child, rather than the child's attainment of specific reading benchmarks. The cognitive element seems to be, at least at the present stage, not very prominent in the RTI model. RTI is primarily a method for early intervention for children "at risk" and for better identification of children who need special education services. At the same time, the RTI model does not include a specific recommendation on how interventions should be shaped. Phase 1 of RTI calls for paying greater attention to children who appear to be "at risk" but otherwise the teaching-as-usual methods are used. Phase 2 of RTI presupposes the implementation of a research-based intervention that can be chosen from a wide range of available programs. Phase 3 calls for individualized intervention attuned to the needs of a specific child, an intervention constructed by the local pedagogical team. The LP assessment on the contrary aims at identifying specific learning abilities and disabilities and includes recommendations regarding cognitive interventions that can help children to enhance their LP.

The sequence of stages in the LP assessment and RTI are also different. LP assessment follows the test–teach–test sequence either in the "sandwich" or the "cake" format. RTI uses the teach–test–teach sequence, with children first provided with reading intervention and then assessed in terms of their progress toward the reading benchmarks. Finally, LP assessment and RTI work on different timescales. LP assessments including the learning phase range from one hour for such specific language assessments as DASS (Hasson, 2018) to 12–15 hours for the entire Feuerstein's LPAD battery (Feuerstein et al., 1979). Interventions here are used for identifying the LP of children and for formulating recommendations regarding the required long-term cognitive and educational interventions. Interventions in the RTI model, on the other hand, are for weeks and months, while periodic assessments are included for monitoring the progress made by children.

Relationships between Learning Potential Assessment and Intervention

One may ask, however, if instead of starting the intervention and then evaluating its results (as in the RTI model) it would not be better to use the LP assessment as a predictor of the effectiveness of a specific type of intervention with a given group of students. Exactly this question was posed by Gellert and Arnbak (2020) in their research on word structure learning (morphology) by 11- to 12-year-old students in Danish schools. The study included the following components:

Pre-test (definition of words).
Static and then dynamic assessment of students' morphological analysis of pseudowords.
Intervention: twenty-four lessons targeting word morphology.
Post-test (definition of words).

One of the main research questions of this study was the ability of the dynamic assessment to predict the students' RTI beyond the impact of their pre-test static measures of the definition of words and morphological analysis.

The pre-intervention and post-intervention tests focused on students' definitions of the two types of words: words already learned by students and the so-called transfer words – words that have not been taught. The words were presented to students in written and spoken form and the students were asked to explain the meaning of the test words orally. The test words included derived words and compound words. To assess the generalization and application of the principles of word morphology, students were also presented with so-called transfer words. The roots and affixes of the transfer words were included in the morphological intervention program, but in combinations other than in the test words.

After the definition of words pre-test, the students' ability in morphological analysis was evaluated in a static and dynamic format. During the static assessment phase, students were presented with twenty untaught morphologically transparent pseudowords in written and spoken form and were asked to define each of them. The pseudowords had been constructed by adding prefixes and suffixes to high-frequency roots (e.g. "wifeless"). The examiner explained to students that they should try to determine and explain the meaning of some made-up words. Two practice items were given to students with correct/incorrect feedback. In the test itself, if the student provided a correct definition of the pseudoword, they were further asked how they know the meaning of this word. If the definition of the pseudoword was incorrect, students were presented with the next pseudoword. As a result of the static phase, the examiner had for each one of the students a list of pseudowords that he/she defined correctly and those that were defined incorrectly. The list of incorrectly defined pseudowords provided the basis for the dynamic phase of the assessment.

During the dynamic phase, the examiner readministered all the pseudowords the student answered incorrectly during the static assessment phase. When the student gave a correct response, the response was acknowledged as correct and the next item that the student had failed during the static assessment was presented. When the student gave an incorrect answer the first of the three prompts was given (see later in this chapter). If the first prompt did not help, the second prompt was given; if this also did not help, the third prompt was given. When the correct response was absent after three prompts, the student was given the correct answer and the procedure started again with the next pseudoword.

Prompt 1 included the request for the student to segment the target word (e.g. "wifeless") into meaningful units (morphemes). If the student identified the parts correctly (e.g. "wife" and "less") the examiner asked the student to define the word by using the meaning of these parts. If the student now provided a correct definition, the examiner presented the next pseudoword the student had failed to identify in the static phase of the assessment. If the student did not respond correctly, the second prompt was given

Prompt 2. The examiner identified the morphemes of the target word (e.g. "wife" and "less") and asked the student to define the word utilizing these parts. If the student provided a correct definition, the examiner presented the next pseudoword, if not, the examiner moved on to the third prompt.

Prompt 3. The examiner presented and explained to the student the morphological structure of another word (e.g. "homeless"). The examiner's elaboration included the analysis of the word structure: The word has two meaningful parts – "home" and "less" – and the operation of combining these parts to arrive at the meaning of having no home. After such an elaboration, the examiner asked the student to return to the question about the word "wifeless." If the student answered correctly, the examiner presented the next pseudoword, if not, the examiner provided the correct answer ("wifeless means having no wife") and then presented the next item.

The intervention included twenty-four lessons aimed at introducing students to basic concepts of morphology, teaching them to segment words into morphemes and to form compound words. Students were also taught about derivational prefixes, suffixes, and compound words.

The results of Gellert and Arnbak's (2020) research indicated that 29 percent of the students demonstrated a rather poor RTI (more than 0.5 SD below the group mean). Moreover, the strongest predictor of the good vs. poor responder status was the static assessment score of the morphological analysis of pseudowords. This in itself is an interesting result because it shows that it is not the level of knowledge about the meaning of the "real" words at the pre-test but the ability to perform and apply the morphological analysis of pseudowords that predicted the students' level of RTI. In other words, analytic cognitive skills proved to be better predictors of learning than the existing word knowledge. But what about the dynamic procedure? The results show that the dynamic assessment score added a modest 4 percent to the static predictor. This result, however, may mainly reflect the way the dynamic score was calculated by Gellert and Arnbak. The dynamic score included both the students' static score and the additional points students received after responding to prompts. Not surprisingly there was a very strong correlation between students' static and dynamic scores because the latter included the former. It would probably be more relevant to compare the predictive power of the static scores and response to prompts scores for those students who received prompts.

Something of this nature had been accomplished in the research of Kozulin (2005). Immigrant primary school students were pre-tested using the static and dynamic assessment with the Raven Colored Matrices test.

After this pre-intervention testing, the students received five weekly lessons of the Feuerstein et al. (1980) cognitive intervention program (see Chapter 5) for a period of nine months. At the end of the school year, the students were post-tested using the static Raven Colored Matrices test. The results demonstrated that the dynamic pre-test was a much better predictor of the students' RTI than their static pre-test results.

Formative Assessment

The last topic to be discussed in this chapter is the relationship between LP assessment and formative assessment. With the wisdom of hindsight, one can discern some common elements in these approaches, and yet in the pivotal paper of Black and Dylan (2009) that defined the main parameters of formative assessment, there is no reference to LP or dynamic assessment. Moreover, even in a recent formative assessment handbook (Andrade et al., 2019) one does not find any discussion about the common elements of these two approaches. This lack of connection might be explained by the initially very different focus of dynamic and formative assessments. The idea of formative assessment has been and still is firmly embedded into the problems of curricular teaching of so-called regular students. The main opposition here is between summative assessment, which evaluates the students' already acquired curricular knowledge and ranks them according to the achievement criteria, and formative assessment, which uses the exam results for changing the instructional process. First of all, this changes the relationships between assessment and instruction. A more traditional summative assessment appears to be set apart from the instructional process itself. Instructional and learning processes have their own features and logic and then at the end of a certain period (e.g. at the end of the semester) a new element – an exam – is added. Such an exam does not really belong to the instructional process but only evaluates its "final" results. Formative assessment on the contrary is firmly embedded into the instructional process; it is performed periodically and its role is not to evaluate the "final" products of learning but to use the exam results for introducing changes into the instructional process itself. The role of students is also different. The results of summative assessment are often just delivered to students as final "fact." There is little that students can do with these exam scores apart from learning what their place is vis-à-vis the class or school average. The results of formative assessment exams are expected to be analyzed jointly by teachers and students so that students are given an opportunity to identify their strong and weak points and to adjust their learning strategies, while teachers use these results to change their instruction. In some versions of the formative assessment, students are encouraged to construct and periodically perform their own self-evaluation. Apart from improving learning strategies, such activity may enhance students' metacognitive skills.

In the field of LP, the main opposition is between static assessment, which evaluates the students' current performance (mainly in cognitive areas), and dynamic assessment, which aims at identifying students' LP. So, in this sense, summative assessment can be viewed as one version of a static assessment. The relationships between formative assessment and LP assessment are more complicated, even if we put aside the difference between cognitive vs. curricular focus. While formative assessment uses the static exam results for implementing instructional changes, LP assessment changes the assessment situation itself by including the teaching/learning phase in the assessment procedure.

The formative assessment model presupposes that after teaching, for example, a math curriculum in a certain way for two weeks, the teacher gives a static math exam that covers the taught material. After analyzing the results of the exam, the teacher concludes which elements of his/her instructional approach should be changed so that the student's learning is improved. This circle of teaching and evaluating is repeated again and again in the hope of achieving the optimal instructional strategy.

The dynamic math assessment is different. The assessment includes prompts or mediation so that its results can help the teacher to identify those math topics that are already fully mastered by a given student, those that are situated in his/her ZPD, and those that are still not in the student's "pipeline." Moreover, the dynamic assessment may provide information about the nature of prompts (e.g. verbal, numerical, graphic) that are more effective for a given student. Based on this LP map, teachers can design their instructional strategies.

In view of the differences outlined here, what can still be defined as common ground for formative and dynamic assessments? The first common feature is the belief in the dynamic nature of the teaching–learning process. Neither teachers nor students are perceived as "static" participants of this process: Both the learning strategies of students and the instructional strategies of teachers can and should be modifiable. The second common feature is a closer integration of the assessment and intervention processes. In the LP field, this is achieved via dynamic assessment that is used as a basis for educational intervention, in the formative assessment field the same integration is achieved by performing periodic assessments that inform changes in the teaching–learning process.

There appears to be enough common ground to envisage a possible alliance of these two approaches in the not-so-remote future. The prerequisites of such a development include, on the one hand, further development of dynamic assessment methodology in curricular areas and, on the other hand, the recognition on the part of formative assessment specialists that dynamic assessments provide information that is much more closely aligned with their formative goals than typical curricular exams that are only interpreted in a formative way.

CHAPTER 5

Cognitive Education and Concept Formation

From Retrospective to Prospective Education

It became a cliché to say that school should prepare children for the future and that one of the important elements of schooling is "learning how to learn." The question is how to turn this general thesis into concrete educational practice. After all, only the most radical of the educational approaches claimed that children are born with all the necessary learning skills and what they need is just maturation and the material for their own learning. Traditional education was quite aware that children are not born with all the necessary learning skills and that formal education includes the process of acquisition of various learning skills. However, these learning skills were taught in the context of what one may call "retrospective" education. Traditional education responded to the important goal of transmitting an unambiguous cultural tradition from generation to generation. It is in this sense that traditional education was retrospective. It took for granted a certain model of the world and a certain cultural tradition. Students were expected to absorb this tradition and a set of intellectual tools associated with it. As a result, schools prepared students to cope with the problems of the past, problems that already had well-known solutions. Of course, some of the skills associated with traditional education, such as reading, writing, and numeracy, are not only valuable but hopefully will remain an integral part of any educational model for years to come. The problem with traditional education is that these skills were firmly embedded in a specific cultural tradition. Learning to read meant being able to read specific texts. Learning to write meant being able to produce specific samples of text, and learning to do math meant only specific math skills. What, then, about the skill of reading a new type of text that one never encountered before? What about adjusting your writing to an entirely different audience? What about understanding a new math problem rather than just solving a limited range of existing tasks?

All these questions became topics of educational discussions for two main reasons. The first one is related to the fact that in the age of multicultural classrooms, an unambiguous cultural tradition cannot be taken for granted (Ardila, 2021). Traditional education tacitly assumed that the literary texts studied at school are similar to the books that students find in their homes. The language used by teachers was expected to be the same language in which parents communicate with their children. Even some of the major historical events were assumed to be common knowledge so only their various interpretations deserved to be included in the school curriculum. These assumptions are not valid for the multicultural classroom. It turned out that a lot of learning that traditional education assumed to be naturally occurring (e.g., enhancement of a child's vocabulary through everyday conversations of children with their parents) had to be deliberately constructed because the language of school does not necessarily correspond to the language of home. In other words, rather than acquiring learning skills in the context of reading, children should be taught learning skills so that they can learn to read.

The second reason for the insufficiency of "retrospective" education is accelerated and pervasive technological innovation that is turning the future into a much more uncertain and dynamic world than ever before. In a sense, educational systems are facing the paradoxical task of preparing students for future activities whose parameters are still unknown at the time of the students' learning. So, instead of preparing students for solving known problems, education finds itself in a paradoxical position where it is called on to prepare students for tasks that are yet unknown. Education is expected to prepare students for the future, but the requirements of future life tasks and occupations are still unknown. "Learning to learn" appears to be the key to switching from retrospective to prospective education. As early as 1985, Chipman and Sigal (1985, p. 1) foresaw the need for prospective education: "In a rapidly changing technological environment, it is difficult to predict what knowledge students will need or what problems they will have to solve 20 years from now. What they really need to know, it seems, is how to learn the new information and skills that they will require throughout their lives."

Let us consider the most desirable qualities of a good student in a traditional educational system. These qualities include the ability to follow the model presented by the teacher, recall and perform standard operations, and remember a large amount of factual information. Exactly the same qualities would also help students to receive high scores in IQ tests and college admission exams like the SAT. Would we claim that these qualities are unimportant? Of course not! All of them are important, but they are also insufficient. In the traditional school, the qualities that went beyond those of a "good student" were only required by a minority of high school graduates who aspired to embark on an academic career. By definition, scholars cannot just follow the already established models, perform standard operations, or succeed just because they have an excellent factual memory. By choosing an academic career, scholars accepted the requirement of not only constantly learning but also learning how to learn better.

In the prospective education model, these "scientific" qualities are required by almost every high school graduate aspiring to succeed in modern society:

> One of the basic skills for success in the knowledge society is the ability to learn. With increasingly rapid changes in the work place, in part due to changing technology and as a result of changing societal needs in the context of globalization, citizens must learn to learn in order that they can maintain their full and continued participation in employment and civil society or risk social exclusion. In this context learning to learn is a quintessential tool for lifelong learning and thus education and training need to provide the learning environment for the development of this competence for all citizens including persons with fewer opportunities (those with special needs and school dropouts), throughout the whole lifespan (including pre-school and adult learners) and through different learning environments (formal, non-formal, and informal). (Hoskins and Fredriksson, 2008, p. 5)

If just learning to read, write, and solve standard math tasks is insufficient, what kind of learning is required for prospective education? One of the possible answers to this question is to focus on more general cognitive skills rather than narrow, content-oriented skills. Thus, there is a need for a "thinking skills" approach.

Thinking Skills Programs: Stand-Alone vs. Infusion

The very first question facing educators who wish to teach thinking skills to their students is: Should we allocate special lessons to the development of thinking skills using specially designed cognitive tasks or should the thinking skills strategies be infused into curricular lessons? This controversy shaped many of the thinking skills discussions (Costa, 2001).

This is how Feuerstein et al. (1980, p. 120) defined the need for separate, stand-alone thinking skills programs:

> The content-free structure of our instruments was determined in response to four major resistances that, in our consideration, impede the use of

curricular content learning for enhancing and modifying cognitive behaviors. The first resistance is of the learner ... The second resistance is that of the material and of the content. The third is the resistance of the teacher, and the fourth resistance is generated by a previous experience of failure.

Though Feuerstein primarily had in mind resistances associated with the education of culturally different students who underachieve, his arguments do not appear to be relevant for teaching thinking to just this specific group. In what concerns learners and their previous experiences, Feuerstein argued that many underachieving students have a previous negative experience associated with particular curricular areas. Some of them already decided that they "fear mathematics" or "despise literature." An attempt to go deeper into the cognitive aspects of math or literature tasks, in Feuerstein's opinion, can only generate greater resistance on the part of students. The stand-alone programs with tasks that are noncurricular offer a chance for breaking the link between the students' previous experience of failure and their current position. This new position is created by the fact that stand-alone programs are new to everyone and that the previous educational reputations are not particularly important in this new context.

In what concerns the material, Feuerstein argued that as curricular learning has its own structure and flow, teaching thinking should also have its own structure and sequence of instruction. Mixing these two structures and sequences, in his opinion, will only weaken both of them. That is why Feuerstein suggests that a stand-alone program should have its own material and tasks that focus exclusively on the development of thinking skills and strategies. Once these skills are firmly established in the students' minds they can be "bridged" to curricular material.

In Feuerstein's opinion, the resistance of teachers is associated on the one hand with their disciplinary affiliation and on the other the pressure of school administration "to cover the curricular material." In what concerns disciplinary affiliation, the math or literature teachers are committed to the logic of their disciplinary instruction and are not comfortable deviating from this logic in favor of cognitive teaching. The infusion of cognitive skills into curricular teaching places an extra, heavy burden on teachers' shoulders who should flexibly insert cognitive elements into otherwise disciplinary-structured material without disrupting the flow of curricular teaching.

So, in Feuerstein et al. (1980) opinion thinking skills should be taught using specially designed cognitive tasks, these tasks should be taught during separate "thinking skills" lessons, and teachers who give these lessons should be properly trained in both the didactics of cognitive education and in the technique of "bridging" cognitive strategies to curricular areas.

Feuerstein's objections notwithstanding, there are several reasons for favoring an opposite approach: the infusion of thinking skills into curricular lessons. Some of these reasons have been elaborated on by Swartz and McGuinness (2014). The first of them is related to the process of what Feuerstein called "bridging." Swartz and McGuinness argued that when thinking skills are taught during separate lessons, the problem of transferring these skills to more specific areas of learning becomes problematic. They expressed doubts regarding the readiness of curricular teachers for finding a place for "bridging" exercises during curricular lessons. When thinking skills are taught by a different teacher during separate lessons these skills don't "belong" to the curricular lessons. In Swartz and McGuinness' opinion, when effective "bridging" between the thinking skills lessons and the disciplinary content lessons does occur, such an instruction actually resembles the infusion approach. In other words, the infusion model expects all subject teachers to embed cognitive elements in their curricular teaching so that these elements do not appear as coming "from the outside" and the teachers become truly responsible for them.

The infusion approach, at least in the form proposed by Swartz et al. (2007), expects teachers to design lessons where thinking skills are added to the curricular content. During these lessons, the students are explicitly introduced to cognitive strategies and then prompted to use these strategies for thinking about the content material they are learning:

> When infusion is accompanied with the introduction of explicit thinking strategies, together with highly scaffolded guidance by the teacher, and prompted reflective metacognition and strategic planning by the students about how they will engage in the same sort of thinking skillfully next time (preparation for transfer), a very powerful learning environment for teaching thinking is created. (Swartz and McGuinness, 2014, pp. 17–18)

To get a better idea of what the infusion lesson looks like, let us consider the following example from the study of Aizikovitsh-Udi (2019). The subject area of the lesson was mathematics and the goal of the lesson was to infuse some critical-thinking skills into learning the concept of the "mediating factor" in statistics. The following critical-thinking skills were targeted: identification of relevant questions and variables, locating the source of information, and evaluating the validity of statements. The high school students were presented with the following statements (Aizikovitsh-Udi, 2019, p. 6):

STUDENT A: "There is a connection between shoe size and level of mathematical knowledge."

STUDENT B: "Can't be."

STUDENT A: "Go to the school in the next building and see for yourself."

STUDENT B: "You are right, the kids who wear bigger shoes really know math better!"

Initially, most of the students participating in this study had a strong intuition that the causal connection between shoe size and mathematical knowledge was impossible, but they did not yet know how to explain and support this intuition. After the preliminary discussion, some of the students were sent to a nearby elementary school "to gather evidence." They stopped random elementary school students and asked them about their shoe size and what mathematical topics they were familiar with. This "data-gathering" expedition introduced a critical element into the statistics lesson, with the students validating the reliability of their source by gathering the (seemingly) corroborative data themselves. The ultimate purpose of the lesson was to lead the students to the recognition of the logical fallacy in directly connecting shoe size to mathematical knowledge by realizing that this connection is generated by a mediating element (the child's age).

This example shows that cognitive and metacognitive skills such as critical thinking can indeed be successfully infused into high school curricular material such as the study of statistics. One should pay attention, however, to the fact that thinking skills were not just infused into the pre-existing curricular material. What actually took place was the substantial revision of the original instructional unit "Probability and Statistics in Daily Life." Aizikovitsh-Udi (2019) created a revised version of the unit that combines the hierarchy of topics in probability and statistics with a corresponding hierarchy of topics in critical thinking, so that, as the students progressed in the former, they would also progress in the latter. We return to the issue of curricular material revision as a precondition for successful cognitive education when we discuss the programs focusing on "academic concepts." In the following section, however, we pay closer attention to the construction and implementation of the stand-alone thinking skills lessons.

Instrumental Enrichment as a Paradigm of the Cognitive Education Program

The history of the development and application of Feuerstein's Instrumental Enrichment (IE) program offers us an instructive perspective for evaluating the motives behind the development of thinking skills programs, their structure, and the challenges they face when implemented in schools and clinics. IE is particularly helpful in this respect, not only because it was one of the earliest such programs, but also because the changes in its applications reflected different aspects of what at the beginning of this chapter was defined as the need for "prospective" rather than "retrospective" education.

Initially (see Feuerstein et al., 1980) the IE program was developed as a tool for closing the educational gap between immigrant and locally born students. In this respect, the IE program responded to the multicultural requirement of "prospective" education. Feuerstein rejected the idea that the educational gap between immigrant students (mainly from North Africa) and Israeli-born students can be closed by just offering the immigrants an "extra dose" of Hebrew language lessons. He also rejected the claim made by some psychologists that the immigrant population had an elevated rate of children with special needs who should be placed in special education schools. Feuerstein pointed to two main reasons for the educational gap. The first reason in his opinion was the lack of MLE related to the trauma of dislocation and the disintegration of a traditional extended family. Children who traditionally received some informal instruction from the members of their extended family became deprived of this source. The second reason was the radical difference between the apprenticeship type of education that immigrant children often received in their original community and the concept-based formal education prevalent in Israeli schools. So, in Feuerstein's opinion, immigrant children should on the one hand receive an "extra dose" of MLE, and on the other hand they should be systematically exposed to cognitive tools associated with formal education. The IE program was constructed to respond to these two needs: It included an extensive collection of exercises focusing on general cognitive skills required in formal education while the didactics of teaching these exercises were based on the principles of mediated learning (see Chapter 1).

Let us use the task in Table 5.1 for analyzing the principles on which the tasks in the IE program were constructed. (This task was constructed by the present author especially to illustrate the IE principles; it does not coincide with any of Feuerstein's IE exercises.)

The process of mediation starts with presenting the task to students and asking them "what do you see here?" The goal is to develop the students' data-gathering skills. The students' answers may range from a short "we see some pictures and words" to a more elaborate description of different images and sentences that appear in the task. If some data are missing,

Table 5.1 *Instruction: Create new items using given parameters of change; respond by drawing or writing your answers*

Task	Item	Parameters of change	New item
1	■	Shape and color	
2	(two figures)	Gender, number, and size	
3	A red barn	Type of building and its color	
4	"Jim lives in Chicago"	Tense and number	

the teacher will ask, "are you sure that this is all." After the data are gathered, the next step is to ask students to read the instruction (*Create new items …*). For the students who are more advanced in their work with the IE program, the task may appear without instruction. In this case, after analyzing the elements of the task, the students are asked, "what do you think we should do on this page?" The students are expected to explain in their own words what should be done. The aim of this type of interactive learning is to activate students' cognitive processes and to turn them from passive recipients of information into active explorers of the given data and formulators of possible problems. The role of the IE teacher is to lead students beyond short answers such as "I see here some pictures and words" into systematic data gathering and data analysis. Data gathering and data analysis are accompanied by the teacher focusing students' attention on the symbolic tools that can facilitate these processes, such as a table. The students are led to understand the meaning of column headings (*Item, Parameters of change, New item*) and the role of table rows. Students learn that column headings determine the type of information that appears in various rows of the same column, while different rows constitute different tasks so that the information about the initial items will appear only in the *Item* column, while items themselves will be different in different rows, for example, graphic images or sentences.

The discussion about what kind of problem is posed by this page leads students to understand that the problem is that of transformation. The given item (e.g., a black square) should be transformed into a new item, not at random but according to the given parameters of change. The IE teachers approach the issue of transformation in two ways. The first of them is the analysis of the given task, for example, enumeration of the qualities of the initial item (e.g., a black square) and determining how these qualities can be transformed into a new item that will have a different shape and color. The second way is through the generalization of the transformations identified in specific IE tasks and applying them to the areas beyond IE. One of these more general issues is the difference between explicit and implicit rules and instructions. Explicitly only two parameters of transformation are mentioned in the black square task: shape and color. However, nothing is said about the new shape, except that it cannot be a square. Are there any implicit limitations about the shape? Should it be a geometric shape such as a circle, triangle, or diamond, or can it also be a drawing of a butterfly or a flower? What about the orientation of the new item? Is it implicitly assumed that the orientation of the new item should be the same as that of the initial one? The discussion of the explicit and implicit instructions leads to an even more general question regarding the number of possible correct solutions for any given task. How many answers are possible in the transformation of the black square task? After an appropriate discussion, students are expected to come to the conclusion that there is an unlimited number of correct solutions to this problem because a new item can be of various shapes and various colors so long as it is not a black square. The IE teacher then leads students to the conclusion that not only IE tasks but many other tasks in school subjects and everyday situations vary in the number of possible solutions. Finally, the IE teacher leads the students to a formulation of a general principle: "When confronted with a task I will first check whether it has one correct answer, several correct answers, or an unlimited number of correct answers." The students are encouraged to bring examples of tasks that look similar but have a different number of correct solutions. For example, $13 + ? = 25$ has only one correct solution, while $13 + ? > 25$ has an unlimited number of correct solutions.

Another issue that starts with the analysis of specific IE tasks and leads to a general principle is the possibility of different response modalities or "languages." The majority of students will respond to the black square task by drawing a geometric shape of a different color (e.g., a white triangle). However, theoretically it is possible to respond to this task not by drawing but by writing a phrase: "white triangle." If one of the students selects a written answer, this allows an IE teacher to probe the possible modality limitations implicit in the data about the initial items. For example, for the initial item that is defined verbally as "a red barn" the new item can be presented as a drawing of, let us say, a white mansion, but it can also appear as the phrase "white mansion." However, when the initial item

Table 5.2 *Instruction: Fill in what is missing*

Task	Item	Parameters of change	New item
1			
2		Gender, number, and size	
3		Tense	"Peter lives in New York City"
4		Type of building and its color	

appears as a sentence, for example, "Jim lives in Chicago," and one of the transformation parameters is "tense," there is no possibility to answer in graphic or pictorial form.

After the work with the tasks that appear in Table 5.1 is completed and the general cognitive principles formulated, the IE teacher may offer students the somewhat similar, but in essence very different task that appears here as Table 5.2. If the goal of the tasks in Table 5.1 was to develop students' cognitive skills associated with data gathering, formulation of the problem, operation of transformation, and evaluation of the number of possible correct solutions, the tasks in Table 5.2 aim at mediating to the students the need for critical thinking on the one hand and creativity on the other. The instruction in Table 5.2 is very short and very general: "Fill in what is missing." So, the only cue that students receive from this instruction is that something is missing and that they should fill in this "something." The students thus are expected to critically examine the tasks, advance some hypothesis regarding what should be done in each one of them, and decide what information is missing. The IE teacher leads students to perform a systematic analysis and comparison of the tasks in terms of information present and information missing. The teacher may ask students to construct a table that presents information about the tasks (something like Table 5.3).

Once the data about different tasks are collected, organized, and compared, students are guided to formulate what should be done in each of the tasks. At this juncture, the IE teacher draws students' attention to the fact that while in Table 5.1 the same kind of data and operation were available in each of the tasks, the operation of transformation was supposed to be

Table 5.3 *Analysis of tasks that appear in Table 5.2*

Task	Item	Parameters of change	New item
1	Present	Absent	Present
2	Absent	Present	Present
3	Absent	Present	Present
4	Absent	Present	Absent

performed in each of them. In Table 5.2 the tasks differ in terms of the data present, and as a result, they also differ in what kind of operation should be performed to generate the missing information. Although this activity is mediated with the help of specific verbal and graphic information presented in Table 5.2, the cognitive principle itself is very general. The principle can be formulated in the following way: "Always check whether all the information required for solving the problem is available and whether a proper operation should be chosen, or whether some information is missing and should be added."

Thus, in tasks 1, 2, and 3 of Table 5.2, all information is present, but the required operations are different. For example, in task 1, the initial item and the new item are given, so they should be compared and the parameters of change can be educed. When one black square is transformed into two gray circles, the parameters of change include shape, color, and number. In task 2 all the necessary information is present, but it is different information than in task 1. What is given in task 2 is the new item and the parameters of change. So, one should start with the analysis of a new item (two black female figures) and perform the operation of reverse transformation. If two black female figures were the result of the transformation that involved the parameters of gender, number, and size, then the initial item should be educed as one or more than two male figures of a size that is either larger or smaller than that of the female figures that appear in the new item.

The solutions of tasks 1 and 2 should be contrasted with task 4 in which only the parameters of change are given (type of building and its color). The students are encouraged to think about what is missing in this task and what kind of information should be added before the solution process can start. They should also consider how to use the parameters of change for identifying the type of possible initial or new items. For example, the parameter "type of building" implies that the initial item was a building, while the parameter "color" implies that the color of this building was given. Of course, the whole range of buildings that can be used as an initial item (e.g., villa, barn, skyscraper, etc.) and the chosen building can be of all possible colors, but it cannot be, for example, "a glass table" because the table is not a building and glass is not a color. Once the information about the initial item is added (e.g., "red barn") then the task becomes similar to those in Table 5.1, with the parameters of change used for generating a new item (e.g., "write mansion").

According to Feuerstein et al. (1980), the IE program should be taught during dedicated thinking skills lessons, but the cognitive principles and strategies developed during the lessons should then be "bridged" to curricular subjects. For this reason, Feuerstein argued against using IE-trained teachers exclusively for IE lessons. His idea was to have subject teachers trained in IE so that in addition to giving two to three IE lessons per week these teachers would continue teaching their subjects to which they "bridge" cognitive principles and the strategies that they mediated to their students during the IE lessons. Such an application model assumed that IE teachers would develop "bridging" exercises in their area of specialization.

For example, the strategies of transformation mediated using tasks similar to those in Table 5.1 can be "bridged" to the following reading comprehension task. The students are given several words and asked to compose two sentences using all of the given words: "car David is the Mary riding and the is bike driving."

Many students have no problems with composing the first sentence, for example, "David is driving the car, Mary is riding the bike." However, some of them become "blocked" and cannot compose the second sentence. Here, the strategy of transformation comes to the rescue. The teacher reminds students how during the IE lesson they were able to transform an initial item into a new item according to a specified criterion of change. Then the teacher asks what kind of transformations are possible in the sentence "David is driving the car, Mary is riding the bike." The students create all possible transformations and identify those that are impossible, such as using new words, not using all available words, or connecting incompatible words. This systematic transformation action generates the following possibilities:

Transformation 1: David → Mary
Transformation 2: car → bike
Transformation 3: driving → riding

The resulting sentences are:

1. "Mary is driving the car, David is riding the bike."
2. "David is driving the bike, Mary is riding the car."
3. "David is riding the car, Mary is driving the bike."

After students reject the second and third sentences as impossible, they arrive at the correct sentence via the use of a cognitive transformation strategy.

This "bridging" example connects the transformation strategy to a relatively simple school task. However, the cognitive strategies related to the problem of identifying the possible missing information developed with the help of tasks similar to those in Table 5.2 can be used for "bridging" to more challenging problems. Let us take as an example the following math problem: There are three sacks of apples. In the first sack, there are six apples more than in the second sack. In the second sack, there are two apples more than in the third sack. How many apples are there in these three sacks?

Students who have not developed the cognitive strategies for checking the available information would probably be either entirely confused by this problem or would start performing some math operations (adding, subtracting, etc.) without first understanding the problem and its features. Those with appropriate cognitive strategies will analyze the problem and claim that in the present form, it does not have a specific answer because only the differences between the number of apples in the sacks are given but what is missing is the number of apples in one of the sacks. Some of the students who studied the strategies of hypothetical reasoning on a deeper level may go even further and state that "if we assume that no one of these sacks is empty, then the total number of applies in these sacks will be no less than thirteen (one apple in sack 3, three apples in sack 2, and nine in sack 1)." This is a truly "academic" answer. Why it is "academic" is discussed in the next section.

Cognitively Oriented Preschool Curriculum

Apart from the separate thinking skills lessons and the infusion of thinking skills into the otherwise standard curriculum lessons, there appears to be a third possibility. This possibility is based on the revision of the curriculum itself so that both the curricular tasks and the didactics of their teaching respond to the goal of promoting students' cognitive development.

In the Vygotskian educational model, the redesign of the curriculum along more cognitively oriented lines should start in preschool. A long line of scholars and practitioners affiliated with this tradition have designed several preschool curricula aimed at developing children's cognitive and interpersonal skills. In what follows we describe the curricula developed by Leonid Venger, Olga Diachenko, and Nikolai Veraksa in Moscow and then adapted for English-speaking countries by Galina Dolya (2007).

One of the first concepts used for designing this preschool curriculum is the concept of "sensory standards." The world around young children is rich with objects of different colors, shapes, sizes, and arrangements. From an early age, children develop intuitive ideas about some of these parameters and the words associated with them. Curricula that systematically introduce children to culturally specific sensory standards impose order on this intuitive knowledge. For example, one of the activities is called "Magic Glasses." Children are given "glasses" (actually empty frames) of different shapes: triangular, square, and round. The rule of the game is that a child who wears glasses of a certain shape (e.g., square) can see only square objects. Children then are asked to describe which objects they "see." Later the game becomes more complex when sensory standards associated with both shape and color are introduced. So, the child who wears red square glasses can "see" only those square objects that are red, and does not "see" green, yellow, or blue objects.

It is important to remember that the goal of these activities is not in creating a simple association between the word "square" and a corresponding geometric shape; the goal is to provide children with cognitive tools for analyzing the surrounding world into culturally agreed-upon elements, such as geometric shapes. An additional goal is to develop in the children the ability to assume a certain position and to internalize it, and as a result to improve children's self-regulation. For example, after a certain period of activities with glasses, children are told to abandon the frames and just imagine that they wear red and square glasses and then describe what they "see" around them. Under these conditions, when asked what they see children often ask their teacher: "With glasses or without glasses?" This question indicates that the children have fully internalized an important idea that the world looks different depending on the position, role, or perspective one is taking. So, the development of "sensory standards" takes place simultaneously with the development of such executive functions as cognitive flexibility and inhibition control.

The second concept used in the preschool curricula is "visual modeling." It is closely related to the more general concept of "symbolic tools" that was discussed in Chapter 2. The transformation and internalization of external symbolic tools into inner psychological tools is perceived in Vygotskian theory as one of the main goals of any formal educational system. These external symbolic tools can be as simple as pencil marks and as complex as a physical formula. At preschool age, children start mastering the skill of using symbolic representations as substitutes and models of objects and relationships. For example, a simple game of substitution shown in Figure 5.1 teaches children to represent some features of one set of objects (toy bears) through other objects (circles). By observing and performing symbolic substitution actions, children acquire the concept of a model and learn that the model includes only some of the objects' features: those essential for a given representation. The model in Figure 5.1 represents such features of the toy bears as their number and size while ignoring their shape and color.

Some of the most important tools that children should acquire in preparation for formal learning are "measuring tools." In the preschool curriculum of Dolya (2007), practice starts with such simple tools as sticks, pieces of string, or strips of paper. All these tools are examples of visual models – their material or color is not important, what is important is only their length. Children practice expressing the length of different objects – tables, benches, bookshelves, etc. – in terms of these measuring tools. Then they are given the task of deciding how to select a new piece of furniture or a plant so that it can fit into the available place. Such activity develops children's hypothetical thinking: Without actually moving a piece of furniture or a plant they estimate their possible dimensions using the available measuring tools.

The use of modeling tools is also applied to the development of children's ability to comprehend, analyze, and eventually retell a story. For example, children learn to use brown squares of different sizes to represent bears in the "Goldilocks and three bears" story, a yellow square to represent Goldilocks, different red shapes to represent bowls, beds, and chairs, and a big gray rectangle as a "house." After learning how to use these representations, children start playing "Symbolic Theater." They place three bears and a Goldilocks outside the "house." The teacher starts telling the story while the children show substitute shapes that are "involved" in a given episode. At the next stage, children are encouraged to match the episode model with an episode picture (from the book). Figure 5.2 shows an episode model representing Goldilocks as she tastes the porridge from three bowls. Children are asked to select one of the pictures from the book that matches the model. This activity continues until children are capable of matching each one of the episode models with the relevant picture.

Figure 5.1   Visual-spatial symbolic modeling of "Goldilocks" characters
(from Dolya, 2007, p. 26, © Galina Dolya, reproduced by permission)

Figure 5.2   Visual-spatial symbolic modeling of "Goldilocks" episodes
(from Dolia, 2007, p. 89, © Galina Dolya, reproduced by permission)

The next stage is to provide children with eight empty frames associated with eight episodes of the story and ask them to fill in each frame with the relevant episode model. In this way two goals are achieved: First, children receive visual support for remembering and then retelling the story; and second, children learn how to use abstract symbolic tools as mediators between the external material (a story) and their own mind (memory of the story). Such modeling activities pave the way to the acquisition of literacy as an activity in which symbolic forms, letters, words, sentences, and texts stand for sounds, actions, events, and emotions.

Preschool Program and Cognitive Control

As already mentioned, one of the crucially important prerequisites of formal learning is the development of so-called executive functions, in simple words the ability to focus and not to be distracted by irrelevant stimuli, to hold information in the memory while performing some operation, and to be flexible. It turned out that the program Tools of the Mind (Bodrova and Leong, 2007) is quite effective in developing executive functions in preschool children and thus preparing them for a successful start of formal schooling (Dimond et al., 2007). Activities in the Tools of the Mind program correspond to those associated with the developmental sociodramatic play period (see Chapter 3) and include role play, acquisition and internalization of symbolic tools, and use of private speech for self-regulation. For example, in one of the activities, called "Buddy reading," one child is expected to tell a story while turning the book pages and pointing to the relevant pictures. The other child is expected to listen to the story. To develop children's ability to self-regulate and switch roles when required, one child was given a drawing of lips and the other one the drawing of an ear. It was explained to the children that "lips talk, ears don't talk, ears listen." These external symbols helped children to stay within their role as long as they had an appropriate symbol and to switch roles following the change of symbols. After a few months, there was no longer any need for supporting symbols; children internalized both roles and the mechanism of switching them. At the next stage, the "listener" was entrusted with the role of asking the "reader" a question about the book after the reading was over. The "readers" in turn internalized the routine of questions and after they finished reading asked themselves about the book to verify their own comprehension.

Private speech that is not intended for communication also helps to improve children's self-regulation. During the activities of the Tools of the Mind program, children were encouraged to use their private speech. For example, in the "Pattern Movement" game, children were shown a pattern of shapes, such as triangle, square, triangle, square, square, triangle, and were asked to respond to each one of the shapes by specific movement, for example, clapping hands to triangle and raising hands to square. Then the required movements were changed and then changed again. Children were taught to keep the present instructions in their working memory and inhibit the previous set of actions. Private speech that was encouraged, but not taught by the teachers, helped children to regulate their behavior. For example, they first said to themselves "clap" when triangle was pointed to, and then actually clapped hands.

Research on the effects of the Tools of the Mind program was conducted in the northeast USA in twenty-one preschool groups of children from low-income families (Diamond et al., 2007). The comparison program was the Balanced Literacy curriculum developed in the school district itself. Both programs had the same content, but only Tools of the Mind was based on Vygotsky's theory and specifically targeted children's self-regulation. Two executive functions tests were used: the Dots Task and Flanker Task. In both tests, motor response to visual stimuli was complicated by an incongruent context. For example, in the Dots Task a flower appearing on the left side of the screen should be responded to by pressing the right-side button. In the Flanker Task the target shape (e.g., triangle) appeared inside an irrelevant shape (e.g., circle). Children were asked to respond ("Which shape is on the INSIDE?") by pressing either the circle or the triangle button. The correct response requires inhibition of attention to the irrelevant, "outside" shape and focusing only on the "inside" shape. The results of the study indicated that children who participated in the Tools of the Mind program outperformed those who were in the Balanced Literacy curriculum in both executive functions tasks. Moreover, it turned out that some of the important academic performance measures such as "get ready to read" scores are significantly correlated with the executive functions' performance.

Cognitively Oriented School-Age Programs

As mentioned in the "Elementary School Age" section of Chapter 3, the elementary school period was perceived by Vygotskians as particularly appropriate for positioning formal learning as children's leading activity. It is important to remember that when Vygotskians wrote about learning as a leading activity they did not mean a generic type of learning that appears as a subordinate element in practically all human activities. Of course, learning takes place during play, practical activity, or interpersonal interaction. What is meant by learning as a leading activity is a specially designed activity of formal learning that aims at turning a child into a self-regulated learner. Learning here does not serve as the means for achieving some other goal – playful, practical, or interpersonal – but as both the means and the goal in itself. This is a period that is particularly suitable for developing "learning for the sake of learning." The key element in this process is the development of children's *reflection* or metacognition.

Zuckerman (2004) identified three main aspects of reflection: (1) the ability to consider the goals, methods, and means of one's own and other people's actions and ideas; (2) the ability to understand other people's point of view and approach things from the perspective other than one's own; and (3) the ability to understand and examine oneself, identifying one's own strong points and limitations.

Each of these aspects of reflection can be developed using a corresponding set of educational activities. The development of the ability to consider goals, methods, and means of action is supported by the use of symbolic tools (signs, symbols, models, and other schematic representations) that help to transform external actions into internal mental schema (see Chapter 2). The process of learning how to use schematic representations starts during the kindergarten period, but only in elementary school does it reach its full realization. That is why some elements of algebra, for example, are taught in "Vygotskian" schools much earlier than in other educational settings – children in these schools are already fully familiar with the advantage of using various symbolic representations for forming inner mental schema of the problem.

The development of the ability to see things from the point of view of others is supported by the activities of peer tutoring, collaborative learning, and teaching younger pupils. In all these activities the emphasis is on the need to look at the object, process, or problem from the perspective of a different person. Teaching younger students, for example, helps older children to articulate some assumptions that for them are "obvious" but exactly for this reason are poorly articulated. Collaborative learning creates conditions for comparing different problem-solving strategies and developing argumentation skills. Zuckerman (2004) emphasized that while actions with objects (words, shapes, numbers, signs, etc.) are explicitly taught to elementary school students, the ability to view the problem from the perspective of others is created indirectly by shaping classroom situations that require collaboration, understanding of an alternative point of view, and its critique.

The ability to examine one's own performance is developed by activities that include choosing criteria of evaluation, building evaluation scales, and considering the "weight" and importance of each performed task. These activities help to demystify the issue of evaluation. Evaluation ceases to be seen as a subjective act of a teacher's or other students' judgment and becomes a process based on clearly identifiable principles and parameters. Children learn how to build different scales and other evaluating devices and use them for self-evaluation. The vague feeling of "I am good at" and "I am poor with" is replaced by a much more articulate evaluation of specific skills and performances. This aspect of the Vygotskian educational approach has a certain affinity with the students' self-evaluation as described in the formative assessment model (Black and Wiliam, 2009).

Lessons in the Vygotskian classroom always aim at identifying some general principles and the limits of their applicability. Already in the first grade, 6- to 7-year-old children who study Russian are encouraged to formulate some general principles rather than just memorize the correct spelling. The teacher provides them with several words and asks them to identify a spelling problem common to all these words. (Russian spelling is more complicated than, for example, German or Spanish.) Children then formulate the general rule applicable to all these words and present this rule as a graphic model. The next stage of the lesson includes the application of the formulated model to additional words. Using information from all these stages, children are expected to convince their peers that the model they developed is correct. Zuckerman (2004) claimed that one of the main changes between the first and the fourth grade can be observed in children's attitudes toward the proposals made by their peers. The first-grade children are still mostly "centered" on their own opinion. If the proposal of other children is different, it is automatically regarded as incorrect. By the fourth grade, children are ready to accept the initial proposals of other children and analyze them in terms of the available data. So, when they reject a proposal made by their peers they do this by comparing the initial hypothesis with additional language data that were not taken into consideration by their peers.

As an illustration of the Vygotskian curriculum let us consider the following mathematics lesson in the first-grade classroom described by Zuckerman and Venger (2010). During the previous lesson, students were introduced to the three main concepts essential for the construction of the number line: Origin (or starting point), Direction of the line, and Unit (also called measuring unit). The students have already acquired some terms in the language of the classroom interaction, such as a "trap." When students suspect that some problem does not have an obvious answer or does not have an answer at all, they warn their peers about the possible "trap." This in itself is already an important critical reasoning skill: The task given by the teacher is not accepted unconditionally as solvable but is evaluated for a possible "trap."

The current lesson started with the teacher reminding students about Origin, Direction, and Unit as essential elements of the number line, and then asking them to solve the problem using the drawing that appears here in the upper part of Figure 5.3. The task was to find the Origin, the Direction of the number line, and the Unit when only two number points

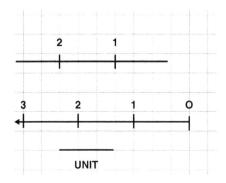

Figure 5.3   First number line task (upper drawing) and its solution (lower drawing)

are given: 1 and 2. Children rather easily solved this problem using the available information about the location of numbers 1 and 2 (see drawing at the lower part of Figure 5.3). They identified the direction of the number line (right to left), they placed the Origin at o, and defined the Unit as the length of three grid squares. Contrary to typical teaching of the number line based on the line with the left to right direction that has o already marked, here the students were taught to construct the line rather than use it as a ready-made product. The students also identified the Unit which does not coincide with a side of the grid square. The latter fact is important because many of the children's typical mistakes stem from the confusion between the Unit of the number line and the square of the grid paper they use.

The truly interesting part of the lesson, however, started when the teacher presented the students with a new problem. She asked them to draw the line, mark the place for digit 3 more or less at the center of the line, then count three grid squares to the right and mark the place for digit 5 (see Figure 5.4 upper). At this moment students spontaneously and without the teacher's prompting started voicing their reflections regarding the task: "five?" "minus" (means that this is impossible), "there is no minus, plus" (plus means that it is possible), etc. The teacher then asked students what is missing in this number line. One of the students said that the Direction is missing, others that digit 4 is missing, some others that it is not only 4 but also other numbers, and then all students together: "origin and unit are missing." The teacher's decision to ask students to draw the line and to place numbers is important because it turned students into "collaborators" in posing the problem. Now, when they are asked to "add what is missing" they solve not just the teacher's but also their "own"

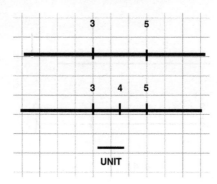

Figure 5.4   Second number line task (upper drawing) and its solution (lower drawing)

problem. The teacher invited one of the students (D) to the blackboard. D claims that there is a "trap" in the problem because it is impossible to place 4 in the middle of the three grid squares that separate 3 and 5. The teacher asked D if he wishes to hear the opinion of other students, and if yes then whom to invite to the blackboard. D invites M, who comes to the blackboard and places the tick mark in the middle of the grid square (Figure 5.4 lower). One of the students (N) objected that one cannot place a tick mark in the middle of the grid square and that the Unit can be either one, two, or three grid squares. Without arguing with N the teacher asked D and M who still stand in front of the blackboard to find the place for Origin. Using the one-and-a-half grid square Unit the boys successfully find the place for Origin. The teacher then asked N if she is ready to solve a really difficult problem. When the girl agreed, the teacher asked her to find a place for 6. N successfully performed the operation using the Unit which she declared to be "impossible" a minute ago. In this way, not only D and M but also N acquired a feeling of the personal appropriation of the correct method.

One may of course claim that this episode is just an example of a good mathematics lesson for first-grade students. Let us, however, focus on what happened during this lesson from a cognitive perspective. Two essential cognitive features became clear from the very beginning of the lesson: (1) The lesson was about construction and not about giving the correct answer, and (2) the cognitive tools that students used were concepts (Origin, Direction, Unit) not just mathematical operations. Procedural knowledge (e.g., how to find the direction of the line) was firmly coordinated with conceptual knowledge. As already mentioned, the first task included a nonstandard direction of the line (right to left), which in itself aimed at developing the students' critical reasoning and cognitive flexibility. The requirement to identify the line unit (which does not correspond to that of the grid paper) not only responded to the important scientific goal of learning about units of measurement, but also to a more general cognitive goal of learning to go beyond the perceptually given (grid paper) and impose your own conceptual tool (Unit) on the given material. During the second part of the lesson, the strategy of overcoming the perceptually given was further reinforced when students argued about the possibility of having a unit that "cuts" the grid square. However, the most important cognitive goal of the second part of the lesson was to develop in students the ability to identify what should be found in the task. In this lies the main difference between the first task in which the teacher not only presented the material but also defined what should be done, and the second task in which the teacher just asked "what is missing?" without giving any instructions. The ability to examine the material, to identify what is given and what is not, and to define the problem is one of the major cognitive goals of formal education. The number line tasks were just material for developing this important ability in first-grade children. In the Vygotskian school curriculum (Zuckerman, 2004) this ability is further developed throughout elementary and into middle school in all subjects.

Education for Concept Formation

To properly understand the Vygotskian model for revising the school curriculum along cognitive lines we should attend to such a controversial issue as the difference between so-called everyday concepts and academic (or scientific) concepts. This issue was discussed in Vygotsky's (1934/2012) polemic with Piaget. Nowadays the majority of psychologists and educators recognize that children don't come to school with their minds as a *tabula rasa* to be filled with the knowledge supplied by teachers. Children come with their own concepts about time, space, quantities, causality, etc. The question is, what to do with these concepts, many of which don't correspond to scientific notions. In the more radical version of Piaget's theory (Inhelder and Piaget, 1958) children were expected to gradually reach the formal operations stage that allows them to absorb scientific concepts. It was tacitly assumed that the previous "prescientific" concepts will fade away once the scientific notions are acquired. When "prescientific" and scientific concepts are presented as belonging to different stages of child development, there appears to be no conflict between them. However, since the time of these early ideas of Piaget, it became clear that many of the "prescientific" concepts persist in the reasoning of adolescents and adults and appear in a form of misconceptions identified by their teachers (see Vosniadou, 2008). So, one cannot say that there is no conflict between children's original concepts about time, space, causality, etc. and the concepts taught in school. This conflict was identified early on by Vygotsky (1934/2012) who defined it as a conflict between children's spontaneous everyday concepts and the "academic" (or scientific) concepts belonging to formal education.

Vygotsky indicated that there is a significant difference, even conflict, between spontaneous concepts that children acquire through their everyday experience and that might be adequate for daily life (e.g., "the sun rises in the morning") and the concepts used for scientific and technological reasoning ("what appears as a sunrise is the result of the rotation of the Earth around its axis"). Children bring to the classroom their pre-existing everyday concepts. The task of formal education is to help children to acquire academic concepts and to understand the difference between them and spontaneous everyday concepts. Researchers and educators belonging to the Vygotskian tradition asserted that the acquisition of academic concepts would not happen spontaneously without deliberate instructional activity (Davydov, 2008). Such activity should be carried out in the psychological "space" where students' experientially rich spontaneous concepts meet the teacher's systemically organized academic concepts. The Vygotskian school curriculum is designed to serve as a basis for the development of subject-specific concepts leading to higher forms of reasoning: literary, mathematical, historical, etc. The gap between cognition ("how") and content ("what") is bridged because a properly constructed and taught curriculum leads to the development of students' higher cognitive functions associated with conceptual reasoning.

Some of the early observations made by Vygotsky and his colleagues about the "clash" between everyday experiences and academic concepts became reinforced by the more recent studies on children's reasoning such as those of Kuhn (2009), who demonstrated that children's everyday experiences may interfere with their logical reasoning. Even young children seem to be able to draw correct causal conclusions from the given premises, as long as the problems are "neutral" and unrelated to children's everyday expectations. When, however, the task is easily connected to everyday experience, for example, to such events as the sale of tickets at a fundraising party, even adults tend to abandon orderly causal reasoning in favor of solutions stemming from their life experiences.

The participants in Kuhn's study were asked to evaluate the influence of various "gimmicks" on ticket sales during the hypothetical fundraising party. The following data were provided to the participants:

- The combination of door prizes, a comedian, and costumes generated medium sales.
- The combination of door prizes, an auction, and costumes generated high sales.
- The combination of door prizes, an auction, a comedian, and costumes generated high sales.

The participants were asked how each of the parameters influenced the sales (e.g., "how does [a comedian] influence the sales?"). One can infer a positive causal relationship between an auction and sales by comparing the first and the third combination. At the same time, by comparing the second and third combinations one is expected to arrive at the conclusion that the addition of a comedian does not change the level of sales. The effects of the two other variables are indeterminate.

Despite this rather transparent logic, 83 percent of the participants in Kuhn's study claimed that two or more variables caused increased sales, and 45 percent claimed that three or all four did so. Moreover, the respondents' certainty regarding their answers was high (an overall average of "certain" on a scale from "just guessing" to "very certain"). Prior experiences markedly influenced causal judgments. Participants attributed a causal role to door prizes (83 percent) much more commonly than they attributed a causal role to costumes (33 percent), although the evidence for these two variables was identical. The task performance was also related to the education level, with college graduates outperforming those with lesser education in virtually all respects.

Kuhn's study demonstrated that logical reasoning even when already firmly established is "vulnerable" to the influence of everyday, intuitive reasoning, which sometimes can be quite illogical. So, the issue of "misconceptions" does not belong exclusively to teaching science and mathematics. It is not enough to promote the process of students' conceptual change in scientific domains; logical-conceptual reasoning should be developed in application to quotidian situations as well. The last point leads us to a more general proposal. While it is rather popular to suggest that the "ills" of public education can be cured by making education "closer to everyday life," here we would like to make an opposite proposal: The academic reasoning developed through formal education should be more forcefully applied to the analysis of everyday situations.

Some of the recent events associated with public perception of the COVID-19 pandemic can be used as an argument in favor of "bringing everyday life closer to formal education." As discussed in greater detail by Thompson et al. (2022), the lack of proper understanding of such a basic mathematical concept as fractions may lead to serious misunderstanding by the general public of the danger of various deceases. For example, by focusing on the large number of deaths caused by the flu, some people claimed that COVID-19 is much less dangerous than the annual flu epidemic. Indeed, by mid-March 2020, 22,000 people died of the flu, while "only" 9,318 died of COVID-19. The absolute numbers, however, were deceptive. The total number of people infected by the flu was 36,000,000, while the total number of people infected by COVID-19 was 227,743. The proper understanding of fractions and percentages would then allow us to understand that the flu mortality rate (the number of deaths divided by the number of infections) was 0.06 percent, which is significantly lower than that of COVID-19 at 4.1 percent. This of course is just one example that shows to what extent academic concepts are essential for making properly informed decisions in everyday life situations.

The problem, however, is not only that academic concepts are not sufficiently used in comprehending everyday life situations, but also that many concepts taught at school are far from being truly academic. As demonstrated by Davydov (2008) and his research team in Russia, as well as Karpov (2003) and others in the USA, a considerable number of concepts developed in classrooms are just enriched and extended everyday notions that lack those features that, from the point of view of Vygotskians, constitute the core of academic concepts.

To be truly academic the concept should be:

- *universal* (within its area of applicability)
- *theoretical* (independent of the amount of the student's previous empirical knowledge)
- *generative* (capable of creating different applications)
- *systemic* (related to an entire system of concepts)

Let us demonstrate the main features of an academic concept by using the mathematical concept of a circle as an example. Often the concept of a circle is introduced in the elementary classroom by pointing to various round objects – plates, round tables, wheels – and asking children what is common between them. When students answer that all these objects have a round shape, a teacher draws a circle on the board and explains that this common shape is called a circle.

There is, however, a very different way to introduce the notion of a circle. It starts with a definition: "Circle is a figure created by a movement of a line segment one end of which is fixed in place, while the other is moving." Let us check which one of these two approaches will provide us with a concept that is universal, theoretical, generative, and systemic. The "round objects" definition relies strongly on the child's previous empirical experience with various round objects (thus it is not theoretical) and provides no built-in mechanism for proving its universality because there is no way to know whether all round objects are like plates or wheels. The possible generativity of the "round objects" concept of a circle is based on the similarity between already known round objects (plates, tables, wheels) and a new object: "I would like this cake to be round like a plate." There is also no systemic connection to any other geometric notions.

On the other hand, the "movement" definition of a circle is theoretical because it does not require any previous empirical knowledge of round objects. It is universal and generative, because all possible circles, very large and very small, already existing and only hypothetical, can be generated in such a way. It is also systemic because it connects the notion of a circle to the notions of line segment and movement.

It would be a mistake to think that academic concepts are typical only for mathematics and natural sciences; they are no less important for humanities and social sciences. Let us look at how children can be introduced to the academic concept of "protagonist" during literature lessons. First of all, one may ask why we need this; why not use the intuitive concept of a "hero"? Like many other intuitive concepts, the concept of a hero leaves children with the following (incorrect) assumptions: The hero is a human being; the hero is a positive character ("a good guy"); it is the hero who tells the story; the hero always wins, and so on.

If, however, instead of using an intuitive notion of a "hero" we introduce an academic concept of "protagonist" we can avoid practically all of these incorrect interpretations. Let us define a protagonist as an actor whose action (or inaction) moves the development of a story. Such a definition is *universal* because every story has some development. Where there is no development there is no story, thus somebody or something moves every story. Our concept of the protagonist is *theoretical* because we do not need to know many stories before we use this concept. The concept is *generative* because by using it we can create a wide range of stories with very different protagonists. For example, in fairy tales many protagonists are not human, they are animals or even natural phenomena, and yet their activities move the fairytale forward. The protagonist (e.g., Sherlock

Holmes) is not necessarily the storyteller (Dr. Watson). It is not only action but also inaction (of Hamlet, for example) that can move the story forward. Finally, the protagonist might be a very unsympathetic person (e.g., Macbeth). The academic concept of the protagonist is also *systemic* because it is connected to the concepts of story development, characters, and storyteller.

Once children are introduced to the notion of a protagonist, they can start analyzing some sample stories (e.g.,"Goldilocks"). Children can be shown that if one "removes" one or another of the bears, only a fraction of the story disappears, but if Goldilocks is "removed" the entire story collapses. Children then realize that although Goldilocks' actions move the story, she is not exactly a hero in the sense that her actions are not exactly very positive. After that children may engage in the exercise of assigning different storytellers to the "Goldilocks" story. The perspective from which the story is told changes, but if the protagonist is identified correctly his/her/its role as a mover of the story remains the same. Finally, after the concept of a protagonist is firmly established through the analysis of a couple of stories of a different type, children may be given the assignment to take some story framework and experiment with changing characters, storytellers, and story development. These exercises help to find the "limit" at which the change of the story development may render a given character unsuitable for the role of a protagonist. Children thus learn to distinguish between essential elements of the story – those related to the actions or inaction of the protagonist – and peripheral elements. The next time they are confronted with some story, and not necessarily only in literature, they will start searching for a method to determine what is essential and what is not.

Teaching in the Zone of Proximal Development

The concept of ZPD (see Chapter 4) has become quite popular in psychological and educational literature and not only concerning assessment. Expressions such as "teaching in the ZPD" or "teaching in the Zone" are very fashionable, often without properly describing what is meant. Thus, it is important to remind ourselves that not every interaction between teachers and students is related to ZPD. A mere transmission of information or a rule of action from a teacher to a student definitely has nothing to do with the notion of ZPD.

So, what does it mean to teach in the ZPD? To answer this question, we should respond to the following self-addressed questions:

1. Who and what is involved in the ZPD-related learning situation?
2. What kind of functions or abilities do we want to see developed?
3. How do we know that our ZPD-related teaching/learning is successful?

In a formal educational context, there are three main "participants" in the ZPD-related learning situation: children, teachers, and the task. What is important to remember is that none of these elements can be reduced to another. For example, the task has some objective properties, but it is usually perceived differently by children and their teachers. For example, this is what Perret-Clermont et al. (1999) and her colleagues saw in the experiments on the conservation of liquids tasks by girls from low-SES families. The conservation of liquids task was staged either as a comparison between the experimenter's glass and the girl's glass or as dividing the juice between two identical dolls. In terms of the conservation of liquids, both situations were equivalent, yet the participating girls gave different answers depending on the situation. So, what experimenters perceived as the same cognitive task, the girls perceived as different tasks. The thinking of the child as it appears in an experimental or educational situation is not an "object" that first happened to be in the child's mind and then became visible to the researcher. The thinking process always responds to the situation as it is perceived by the child and constitutes a part of a particular activity in which the child is involved. So, a teacher should, first of all, decide about the activity he or she is staging in the classroom and how this activity is perceived and interpreted by children.

To be related to ZPD the classroom activity should have a developmental goal. This brings us to the second question: What kind of functions or abilities do we want to see developed? Zuckerman (2007) and her colleagues insisted that it is rather misleading to imagine that every child can be developed harmoniously. In her opinion, development in a certain direction always takes place at the expense of other abilities. For example, strong development of metacognitive learning skills does not contribute automatically to the child's moral development or artistic creativity. Even within the typical learning abilities, an ability to follow the teacher and copy his/her action leads children in one direction, while an emphasis on exploratory activity and the critical evaluation of possible "traps" leads them in the other. We discussed some aspects of this dilemma in Chapter 4. The students' abilities to use models, cues, and prompts appeared to be different from their ability to integrate already existing skills for solving a novel problem. To be a quick learner is not the same thing as being a skillful problem solver.

The Vygotskian educational approach that emphasizes the development of reflective and metacognitive skills at the elementary school age made this choice deliberately with a full awareness that some other functions related to a child's personality and artistic creativity cannot be equally developed in the same context. Teaching in the ZPD on a macro level depends on the educators' decision on what kind of functions they want to be constructed at a given developmental period. On the meso and micro levels the same question should be posed in terms of specific activities and tasks given in the classroom. By designing these activities and choosing the tasks, educators should always ask themselves what developmental goal they have in mind, and what exactly they want to develop in children in terms of children's cognition.

From the point of view of Vygotskians, one of the main abilities to be developed in children in elementary school is the ability to learn jointly with adults, primarily teachers. Children's ZPD is therefore defined not so much in terms of children's own cognitive skills, as in terms of inter-active collaborative skills that allow them to request the necessary (and only the necessary) assistance from their teachers. Developmental progress is therefore evaluated according to the degree of sophistication in children's ability to identify what kind of help they need in order to approach, assess, and solve a given problem. So, the popular interpretation of ZPD as a "distance" between problems solved by the child independently and those solved with assistance should be elaborated by adding two additional aspects: How the child requested this assistance and what kind of assistance has been provided by the teacher.

The third question is related to the evaluation of the effectiveness of ZPD-based teaching. Two notions help us to answer this question: the notion of internalization and the notion of students' learning initiative. Internalization is a process by which an interactive learning situation that involves students and teachers becomes an inner "property" of the students themselves. In simple words, what they did together the child is now capable of doing him/herself. If at the previous stage solving the problem required some key questions posed by the teacher, at the next stage these questions are posed by a student to him/herself. In a certain sense, the interactive nature of learning is still preserved, but now as an inner dialogue of a student with him/herself.

Learning initiative is the ability of students to go beyond the practical mastery of the task or an assignment. Let us take the case of literacy. Initiative indicating the ZPD leap is observed when the child extends or combines already learned skills in a direction that cannot be immediately predicted. Consider the following case of a 10-year-old trilingual child (Russian, English, Hebrew) who during his first day in Prague looked at one of the Czech shop signs and commented: "This is a Russian word written in English." (The meaning of the Czech word was indeed the same as in Russian, while Czech letters are Latin rather than Cyrillic.) The child's previous language experience included fluent oral Russian (family language), native level of Hebrew (the language of his education and social environment), and English as a foreign language studied with a private teacher. Though the study of each one of these languages had its own goals and objectives the boy's parents and teachers apparently succeeded in creating conditions for the child's advancement to the next, meta-linguistic level. Instead of just using each language in its concrete, practical context the child went beyond practical context to the "theoretical" level that links word meanings and scripts of various languages.

In a more general sense, success in teaching literacy should be sought not only in the children's ability to decode, retell, or analyze texts given in the classroom but also in their becoming independent, avid readers. Literacy skills create a foundation for the next stage in the child's development: the stage of becoming an independent and enthusiastic reader. Some children will then use their reading skills for various intellectual pursuits, others will enjoy the esthetic quality of literary tests, while yet others may shield themselves from an unfriendly social environment by immersing themselves in the experience of literary fantasy.

So, on the practical level, teaching in the ZPD would require teachers to decide about their goal: what cognitive and interactive abilities they want to develop in their students, what kind of classroom activities support the chosen goal, how these activities are perceived by students, and whether as a result of educational intervention students internalize the target functions and demonstrate initiative beyond the practical application of the learned skills.

Cognitive Education and Teacher Training

Regarding the preparation of teachers for teaching thinking skills to their students, the situation is somewhat paradoxical. On the one hand, the core school curricula in practically all European and North American countries includes "development of thinking skills" as one of their key objectives. On the other hand, not much is known about the effectiveness of teachers' professional development in this area. Interestingly enough the problems with teachers' understanding of what it means to teach thinking apparently do not depend on the type of thinking skills programs: stand-alone, infusion, or cognitive curriculum. For example, in the programs for the infusion of cognitive and metacognitive strategies in curricular teaching, there appears to be a considerable gap between teachers' acknowledgment of the importance of cognitive and metacognitive skills and the teachers' understanding of these skills. It appears to be obvious that for teaching cognitive and metacognitive skills teachers should: (1) have good knowledge about various elements of thinking, cognition, and metacognition; (2) be skillful in analyzing various tasks in terms of their cognitive and metacognitive requirements; and (3) possess pedagogical strategies for mediating this expertise to students. However, as demonstrated in the study of Zohar and Lustov (2018), teachers' acknowledgment of the importance of metacognitive skills in science teaching does not mean that these teachers possessed the necessary knowledge about metacognition or pedagogical strategies for teaching the relevant metacognitive skills to their students.

The need for proper cognitive and metacognitive skills of course is not limited to teachers who teach curriculum-based programs; these skills are no less important for teachers who teach stand-alone cognitive lessons. However, even some of the lengthy professional development programs, such as training teachers in Feuerstein et al.'s (1980) Instrumental Enrichment (IE), though effective in enabling teachers to solve cognitive tasks are less effective in developing their reflective and metacognitive skills. In the study of Kozulin (2021), both the problem-solving and the reflective metacognitive skills of teachers-in-training were evaluated at the beginning and after ninety hours of IE program workshops. The teachers solved a selection of cognitive tasks and were asked to describe their problem-solving strategies. The evaluation of problem-solving strategies included the following parameters: the relevance of the strategy for solving specific tasks, the completeness of the list of all required strategies, and the precision in their description. While the teachers' ability to solve cognitive problems improved considerably from the pre-training to post-training tests, this cannot be said about strategy reflection. Even after ninety hours of the IE workshops the teachers' ability to describe their strategies completely and precisely ranged from 38 percent to 69 percent depending on the type of cognitive task.

In what follows we focus more on the third type of thinking skills training, the one associated with a cognitive curriculum based on the idea of academic concepts discussed in the previous section. One of the important aspects of the cognitive curriculum is to prepare students for critically evaluating the tasks given to them, identifying the missing information, and advancing hypotheses regarding the range of possible solutions.

A group of fifteen female in-service special education teachers participated in the study described here as a part of their MEd program. The notion of academic vs. everyday concepts was taught to them in the context of the course "Sociocultural Theory of Learning" taught by the present author. The course focused on different aspects of Vygotsky's and neo-Vygotskian theories of instruction and learning including the topics of symbolic tools, mediation, ZPD, dynamic assessment, and cognitive curriculum. In addition to the discussion of the notion of academic concepts and cognitive curriculum, the participants had access to the relevant research and didactic literature.

At the end of the course, the participants were given the task that was mentioned earlier in this chapter: There are three sacks with apples. In the first sack, there are six apples more than in the second sack. In the second sack, there are two apples more than in the third sack. How many apples are there in these three sacks?

The participants were asked to imagine that the task was given to a group of children and then respond to the following questions:

1. Some children gave a wrong answer, for example …
2. Some children said that there is no correct solution to this problem. Explain why?
3. Some children gave an "academic" answer, for example …
4. Explain the difference in the reasoning of those children who said that the problem does not have a correct solution and those who gave an "academic" answer.

Participants' responses were coded by two scorers for the appropriateness of answers and the participants' ability to explain the difference between "no correct solution" answers and "academic" answers. In what concerns the question about wrong answers, all participants except one produced appropriate examples of the "wrong answers." Regarding the question about "no correct solution," 60 percent of the participants provided plausible explanations, while the explanations of the remaining 40 percent were inadequate. Explanations were scored as plausible if they referred to the lack of sufficient data for producing one specific correct solution to the problem. Explanations that did not mention the lack of sufficient data were scored as inadequate.

Plausible explanations included the following statements: "Because there is no data necessary to arrive at a concrete answer," "Because there is not one correct answer," "Because the quantities of apples in any one of the sacks are not given."

The inadequate explanations included: "Because children did not use schematic representations," "Because they did not use symbolic relationships," "Because they did not understand the data."

In the question about "academic answers," 47 percent of the participants provided adequate examples of "academic" answers, while the examples of 53 percent were inadequate. The answers were scored as adequate if they referred to the possibility of having a range of correct answers or/and provided a formula for generating possible correct answers.

Adequate examples of "academic" answers included: "X – sack B, X + 6 – sack A, X–2 – sack C. There are several possibilities," "There is an unlimited number of solutions," "In the 3rd sack there is the smallest amount and then it is possible to write an equation."

The most challenging and at the same time most interesting question was about the difference between "no correct solution" and "academic" answers. Only two participants were able to provide a complete explanation of the difference between the failure to find one correct numerical solution and "academic" answers that focus on the possibility of having several correct solutions. These are their explanations: "Children who said that there no correct solution looked for a concrete answer, while [those who gave] academic searched for the relationship between three elements and [understood] the need to have a formula." "'Academic' thinking – an unlimited number [of solutions] vs. everyday thinking – the absence of one specific number."

Two additional participants correctly claimed that the difference is between an everyday and an academic approach ("Difference between everyday and scientific thinking") but failed to properly elaborate their claim.

Explanations offered by the rest of the participants (73 percent) were inadequate, for example: "The first group thinks concretely, while the second abstractly," "Those who understood the use of symbols vs. those who do not," "Scientific used the schema of the tool."

These results suggest that the acquisition of the notion of academic concepts and its implementation in the cognitive curriculum constitutes a challenging task even for experienced in-service teachers. Even the first metacognitive task of explaining the possible reasons for "no correct solution" answers proved to be difficult for 40 percent of participants. They tried to fit some of the concepts they learned in the "Sociocultural Theory of Learning" course, such as "symbols," "tools," and "schema," into the questions that were not related to these concepts. Even more difficult was the task of formulating an "academic" answer to a math problem that had missing data and multiple possible solutions. The higher the metacognitive demand, the more difficult it was for participants to elaborate a complete answer. The greatest difficulty was in comparing the hypothetical "no correct solution" and "academic" answers.

Of course, this study probed the reflective skills of only a small group of special education teachers. However, it still offers an opportunity for identifying some general challenges facing the cognitive curriculum approach. First of all, the results confirm that in-service teachers need a deeper and more elaborate study of the notion of "academic" concepts and their application with concrete school material. The difference between "academic" concepts and children's spontaneous concepts remained a very challenging topic even for experienced in-service teachers. In addition, the results showed that even those teachers who correctly described possible "academic" answers experienced considerable difficulty in elaborating the difference between "academic" and "nonacademic" answers. The latter task is metacognitively more challenging and it appears that this aspect constituted the main difficulty for the participants. One may conclude, therefore, that beyond the task of introducing in-service teachers to some of the notions associated with the theory of cultural mind lies a more general and probably more important task of developing teachers' metacognitive reasoning. In this sense, the challenge is not only for the cognitive curriculum approach but for all approaches aimed at developing students' thinking skills.

Conclusion
Connecting the Dots

As a starting point in this book, we proposed looking at human cognition and learning as sociocultural phenomena. Of course, there are many biological and behavioral functions shared by human beings and animals, but the goal of the sociocultural approach is to focus exclusively on specifically human aspects of the human mind. These specific human abilities are developed under the direct influence of social and cultural factors; because of this, we can talk about the cultural mind.

We proposed looking at the development and the functioning of the cultural mind with the help of the following concepts: mediation, symbolic tools, leading activities, learning potential, and cognitive education. These five concepts are those metaphorical dots that we need now to connect. The concept of mediation serves as a superordinate concept in the theory of the cultural mind because it captures the most important feature of this theory: the role of culture as the mediator between the world and human beings. The world appears to human beings as a cultural world because they don't perceive it in its natural form but as filtered through the prism of mediation provided by other human beings, material and symbolic tools, and various culturally shaped activities. So, culture as a mediator should be further elaborated through its more concrete manifestations. We explored in greater detail three of these manifestations: culture as it shapes the actions of human mediators, culture as it is embodied in symbolic tools, and culture as it appears in various human activities (e.g., formal education). Of course, these three mediational functions of culture are closely interconnected. It is impossible to organize mediation via activities without human participation while such participation often includes symbolic tools. On the other hand, to teach a novice how to use symbolic tools you need an expert human mediator, but by the same token, the quality of human mediation is often enhanced by the use of symbolic tools. So, it is important not only to explore human mediation, symbolic tools, and leading activities but also their interactions.

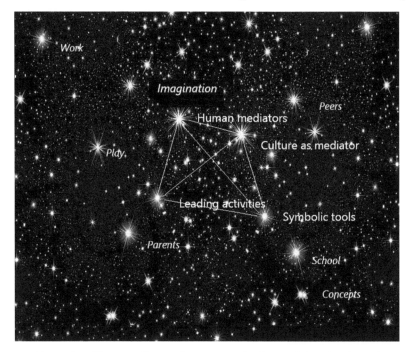

Figure C.1   The constellation of concepts in the theory of the cultural mind

Let us start with human mediation. These days a lot is said and written about the radical changes expected in the field of education and learning, particularly changes related to the digital revolution. In this respect, there appears to be a broad consensus regarding sources of knowledge. In the past, teachers were the primary source of knowledge for their students and one of the main educational activities was the transmission of information from teachers to students. The digital revolution changed this situation. Information became available even in the most remote places as long as they are connected to the internet. This new situation, in our opinion, turned mediation into the main function of the teachers. With the abundance of available information, the need to attract and keep students' attention, to help them to select relevant information and evaluate it, to enable them to move from information to generalization, and to understand the broader meaning of learning acts became of paramount importance. All of these aspects of education and learning are directly related to the criteria of mediated experience discussed in Chapter 1. In a sense, the digital revolution both freed teachers from some of their responsibilities and made their job more challenging. It is easier just to tell students about something that they don't know and have never heard about than to provide them with strategies for finding the relevant information, evaluating it, and thinking about it in a conceptual form. The mediational role of teachers is connected to the changes that should be made in educational systems. Some of the possible guidelines for more developmentally oriented education were discussed in Chapters 3 and 5. Some of the models of developmental education that were created before the digital revolution but focused on students' cognitive and metacognitive skills acquired additional value as a result of this revolution.

We argued, particularly in Chapter 4, that not only teachers but also other educational professionals such as psychologists and speech therapists should act as mediators. By introducing mediation into the practice of cognitive and educational assessment, the nature of assessment is changing. Instead of just checking what children are already capable of doing alone, it becomes possible to evaluate what they can do with the help of a mediator. This in turn helps to identify their LP. What started many years ago as an attempt to offer an LP alternative to static intelligence tests, in recent years spread to such areas as the LP of language, reading, and mathematics. Moreover, the early dichotomy of static assessment vs. LP became replaced by a more varied field including such approaches as formative assessment and RTI that have some affinity with LP.

The digital revolution mentioned earlier had already started having an impact on the area of assessment in general, but what is more important here is that it also influenced the area of LP. In the near future, we will definitely see more research comparing the LP assessments performed by human mediators vs. computer-based LP assessments. One should not forget, of course, that mediation provided in the computer-based LP assessments is not created by computers themselves but by human assessors who use digital technology for implementing their mediational ideas.

The next "dot" to be connected is mediation via symbolic tools. The theory of the cultural mind ascribes particular value to symbolic tools as the agents of change in human behavior and cognition. As discussed in Chapter 2, symbolic tools help human beings to go beyond their immediate experiences. Reading and writing, pictures, maps, and plans help people to experience places and events far beyond their immediate environment. Symbolic tools not only provide a system of representations; they are truly mental instruments in a sense of their function of helping to identify the essence of a given object or event and present it in a condensed, symbolic form. The mastery of symbolic media that serve as a tools of generalization and reflection is therefore a prerequisite for successful education. Throughout this book, but particularly in Chapters 2 and 5, we demonstrated how an early introduction of children to symbolic tools can help them overcome some typical learning difficulties. The acquisition and internalization of symbolic tools rarely happen spontaneously. We thus argued in favor of the systematic introduction of school children to such symbolic organizers as tables, graphs, maps, and plans as tools rather than just elements of content material. It looks as though the current digital revolution has produced an almost paradoxical situation. On the one hand, children seem to be quite skillful in using different icons and images for communication on social media, but on the other, they continue experiencing serious difficulties with such simple tools as tables and graphs. Only deeper learning of the cognitive functions of symbolic tools will resolve this paradox.

The last "dot" to be connected is mediation via specially organized activities. The concept of leading activities elaborated in Chapter 3 can be used in two different ways. It can be used as an alternative perspective on child development as a whole. Instead of viewing the development as an almost automatic sequence of maturational stages, the leading activities theory proposes viewing each developmental period as shaped by leading activities that are socioculturally specific. The leading activities not only differ from period to period, but they also differ from culture to culture. Mediation via activities of course depends on human mediators and symbolic tools, but in our opinion cannot be reduced to them. Not only such a highly structured activity as formal education but also much "softer" parent–child object-centered activities have their own structures. It is these structures that determine the specific features of each developmental period.

The second way of using the concept of leading activity is to focus on specific developmental periods and elaborate on leading activities that characterize each period. In Chapter 3 we paid greater attention to three developmental periods: preschool age, elementary school age, and adolescence. We focused on these periods because, in industrial and post-industrial societies, they coincide with the period during which children find themselves in institutionalized educational frameworks. These frameworks in and by themselves do not determine the leading activities; such activities should be constructed. Of course, different educational models provide different teaching and learning activities. We focused, however, on those models that aimed at promoting students' cognitive and metacognitive abilities rather than just specific curricular skills. During the kindergarten period, these were the skills of imagination, the ability to switch perspectives and roles, and self-regulation. During the primary school period, these were the reflective and critical reasoning skills and the ability to think using academic rather than everyday life concepts. During the period of adolescence, the challenge was to promote higher-level conceptual learning using the students' interpersonal interaction activity as a leading activity.

During each of these periods, the structure of leading activities places particular requirements on human mediation and symbolic tools. Kindergarten teachers are expected to be able to select appropriate symbolic tools and activities so that children can learn how to use symbolic representations of situations and events in symbolic rather than just real-life forms. Similar symbolic tools provided by teachers also serve as mediators that help children to self-regulate during the play activity. During the elementary school period, the mediational role of teachers is essential in promoting conceptual reasoning and metacognition. Teachers are expected to constantly keep in mind not only the curricular but also the cognitive-developmental goals of their lessons. Instead of providing students with the ready-made solution to well-known problems, teachers-mediators are expected to develop students' critical reasoning skills, teach them how to identify problems with multiple correct answers, and lead them to understand the difference between everyday and academic concepts. Each one of these educational goals requires its own collection of symbolic tools, from simple strips of paper as a measuring device to formulae, graphs, and flowcharts. The role of a teacher-mediator in middle and high school is first of all to skillfully use students' interpersonal activities for promoting the development of high-level reasoning and learning skills. The shift from individual to small-group collaborative projects is one of the means for achieving this goal. The symbolic tools suitable for this period ranged from research protocols jointly written as a part of a science experiment project to script and songwriting for students' theater performances.

The network of concepts and relationships presented in Figure C.1 offers an additional symbolic tool that can be used by both researchers and practitioners for further developing the theory and practice of the cultural mind. Each "dot" and each connection are open to further elaboration and development.

References

Ainsworth, M. (1962). The effects of maternal deprivation: A review of findings and controversy in the context of research strategy. In *Deprivation of maternal care: A reassessment of its effects* (pp. 97–163). World Health Organization.

Aizikovitsh-Udi, E. (February, 2019). Construction of Critical Thinking Skills by the infusion approach in "Probability and Statistics in Daily Life". In *Eleventh Congress of the European Society for Research in Mathematics Education*, Utrecht University, Netherlands. Downloaded on September 23, 2022 from https://hal.archives-ouvertes.fr/hal-02421215/document

Alexandrova, E. I. (1998). *Matematika: uchebnik dlia pervogo klassa* [Mathematics: Textbook for the first grade]. Dom Pedagogiki.

Andrade, H. L., Bennett, R. E., & Cizek, G. J. (Eds.). (2019). *Handbook of formative assessment in the disciplines*. Routledge.

Ardila, A. (2021). Cross-cultural differences in cognition and learning. In T. K. Shackleford (Ed.), *The SAGE handbook of evolutionary psychology: Foundations of evolutionary psychology* (pp. 420–435). Sage Reference. https://doi.org/10.4135/9781529739442.n23.

Bannert, S. (2013). A day in the life of a wheelchair user: Navigating Lincoln. *Business Insider*. www.businessinsider.com/what-its-like-to-be-in-a-wheelchair-2013-5.

Barnham, L. (2013). *From hand to handle*. Oxford University Press.

Berk, L., & Winsler, A. (1997). *Scaffolding children's learning*. National Association for the Education of Young Children.

Black, P., & Dylan, W. (2009). Developing the theory of formative assessment. *Educational Assessment, Evaluation and Accountability, 21*(1), 5–31. https://doi.org/10.1007/s11092-008-9068-5. S2CID 55955635.

Black, P., & Wiliam, D. (2010). Inside the Black Box: Raising standards through classroom assessment. *Phi Delta Kappan, 92*(1), 81–90. https://doi.org/10.1177/003172171009200119.

Bodrova, E., & Leong, D. (2007). *Tools of the mind: The Vygotskian approach to early childhood education*. Pearson/Merrill Prentice Hall.

Bodrova, E., & Leong, D. (2015). Vygotskian and post-Vygotskian views on children's play. *American Journal of Play, 7*, 371–388.

Bodrova, E., & Leong, D. (2019). Making play smarter, stronger, and kinder: Lessons from Tools of the Mind. *American Journal of Play, 12*, 37–53.

Brown, A., & Ferrara, R. (1985). Diagnosing zones of proximal development. In J. Wertsch (Ed.), *Culture, communication and cognition* (pp. 273–305). Cambridge University Press.

Buchanan, R. A. (2018). History of technology. *Encyclopedia Britannica.* www.britannica.com/technology/history-of-technology.

Budoff, M. (1987). The validity of learning potential assessment. In C. Lidz (Ed.), *Dynamic assessment* (pp. 52–81). Guilford Press.

Chaiklin, S. (2003). The Zone of Proximal development in Vygotsky's analysis of learning and instruction. In A. Kozulin, B. Gindis, V. Ageyev, & S. Miller (Eds.), *Vygotsky's educational theory in cultural context* (pp. 39–64). Cambridge University Press.

Chipman, S., & Sigal, J. W. (1985). Higher cognitive goals for education: An introduction. In S. Chipman, J. W. Sigal, & R. Glaser (Eds.), *Thinking and learning skills* (vol. 1, pp. 1–19). Lawrence Erlbaum Associates, Publishers.

Costa, A. (Ed.) (2001). *Developing minds.* Association for Supervision and Curriculum Development.

Cummings, V., Jordan, P., & Zvelebil, M. (2018). *The Oxford handbook of the archeology and anthropology of hunter-gatherers.* Oxford University Press.

Davydov, V. V. (2008). *Problems of developmental instruction: A theoretical and experimental psychological study.* Nova Science.

Dehaene S., Pegado F., Braga L. W. et al. (2010). How learning to read changes the cortical networks for vision and language. *Science, 330*(6009), 359–364.

Diamond, A., Barnett, S. W., Thomas, J., & Munro, S. (2007). Preschool program improves cognitive control. *Science, 318*, 1387–1388.

Dolya, G. (2007). *Keys to learning: The Vygotskian approach to early education.* GDH Publishing.

Elkonin, D. (1972). Toward the problem of stages in the mental development of the child. *Soviet Psychology, 10*, 225–251.

Erikson, E. (1962). *Childhood and society.* Norton.

Feng, M., Heffernan, N. T., & Koedinger, K. R. (2009). Addressing the assessment challenge in an online system that tutors as it assesses. *User Modeling and User-Adapted Interaction: The Journal of Personalization Research (UMUAI Journal), 19*(3), 243–266.

Ferrara, R., Brown, A., & Campione, J. (1986). Children's learning and transfer of inductive reasoning rules: Studies of proximal development. *Child Development, 57*, 1087–1099.

Feuerstein, R. (1968a). The Learning Potential Assessment Device. In B. W. Richards (Ed.), *Proceedings of the First Congress of the International Association for the Scientific Study of Mental Deficiency.* Michael Jackson.

Feuerstein, R. (1968b). *The Learning Potential Assessment Device: A new method for assessing modifiability of the cognitive functioning in socio-culturally disadvantaged adolescents.* Proposal presented to the Israel Foundation Trustees. The Youth Aliyah Department of the Jewish Agency.

Feuerstein, R. (1991). Cultural difference and cultural deprivation. In N. Bleichrodt, & P. Drench (Eds.), *Contemporary issues in cross-cultural psychology* (pp. 21–33). Swets and Zeitlinger.

Feuerstein, R., & Hoffman, M. (1982). Intergenerational conflict of rights: Cultural imposition and self-realization. *Viewpoints in Teaching and Learning, 58,* 44–63.

Feuerstein, R., & Rand, Y. (1974). Mediated Learning Experience: An outline of proximal etiology for differential development of cognitive functions. *Journal of International Council of Psychology, 9–10,* 7–37.

Feuerstein, R., Falik, L., & Feuerstein R. S. (2015). *Changing minds and brains.* Teachers College Press.

Feuerstein, R., Rand, Y., & Hoffman, M. (1979). *The dynamic assessment of retarded performer.* University Park Press.

Feuerstein, R., Rand, Y., Hoffman, M., & Miller, R. (1980). *Instrumental Enrichment: An intervention program for cognitive modifiability.* University Park Press.

Feuerstein, R., Feuerstein, R. S., Rand, Y. et al. (2006). *Creating and enhancing cognitive modifiability: The Feuerstein Instrumental Enrichment program.* International Center for the Enhancement of Leaning Potential.

Feuerstein, R. S., Tzuriel, D., Cohen, S. et al. (2019). Integration of Israeli students of Ethiopian origin in Israeli universities. *Journal of Cognitive Education and Psychology, 18*(1), 18–34.

Gellert, A. S., & Arnbak, E. (2020). Predicting response to vocabulary intervention using dynamic assessment. *Language, Speech, and Hearing Services in Schools, 51,* 1112–1123.

Gillam, S., Holbrook, S., Mecham, J., & Weller, D. (2018). Pull the Andon Rope on working memory capacity interventions until we know more. *Language, Speech, and Hearing Services in Schools, 49,* 434–448.

Greenstein, L. (2010). *What teachers really need to know about formative assessment.* ASCD.

Grigorenko, E. (2009). Dynamic assessment and response to intervention. *Journal of Learning Disabilities, 42,* 111–132.

Guthke, J., Beckman, J. F., & Stein, H. (1995). Recent research evidence on the validity of learning tests. In J. S. Carlson (Ed.), *Advances in cognition and educational practice: European contributions to dynamic assessment* (pp. 117–143). JAI Press.

Guttman, L. (1959) Introduction to facet design and analysis. In *Proceedings of the Fifteenth International Congress of Psychology, Brussels 1957* (pp. 130–132). North Holland.

Haeussermann, E. (1958). *Developmental potential of preschool children.* Groune & Stratton.

Hart, B., & Risley, T. R. (1995). *Meaningful differences in the everyday experience of young American children.* Paul H Brookes.

Hasson, N. (2018). *The dynamic assessment of language learning.* Routledge.

Hessels-Schlatter, C., & Hessels, M. (2009). Clarifying some issues in dynamic assessment. *Journal of Cognitive Education and Psychology, 8*(3), 246–251.

Higgins, E. T. (2016). Shared-reality development in childhood. *Perspectives on Psychological Science, 11*(4), 466–495.

Hirsh-Pasek, K., Adamson, L. B., Bakeman, R. et al. (2015). The contribution of early communication quality to low-income children's language success. *Psychological Science, 26*(7), 1071–1083. https://doi.org/10.1177/0956797615581493.

Hoskins, B., & Fredriksson, U. (2008). *Learning to Learn: What is it and can it be measured?* European Commission, Center for Research on Lifelong Learning.

Infante, P., & Poehner, M. (2021). Alex, the toolmaker: Tool-and-result activity in the L2 learning context. *Linguistics and Education, 63.* https://doi.org/10.1016/j.linged.2020.100862.

Inhelder, B., & Piaget, J. (1958). *The growth of logical thinking from childhood to adolescence.* Basic Books.

Kamii, C. (1985). Leading primary education toward excellence: Beyond worksheets and drill. *Young Children, 40*(6), 3–9.

Kaniel, S., Tzuriel, D., Feuerstein, R., Ben-Schachar, N., & Eitan, T. (1991). Dynamic assessment: Learning and transfer abilities of Ethiopian immigrants to Israel. In Feuerstein, R., Klein, P., & Tannenbaum, A. (Eds.), *Mediated learning experience: Theoretical, psychosocial, and learning implications* (pp. 179–209). Freund.

Karpov, Y. (2003). Vygotsky's doctrine of scientific concepts: Its role for contemporary education. In A. Kozulin, B. Gindis, V. Ageyev, & S. Miller (Eds.), *Vygotsky's educational theory in cultural context* (pp. 65–82). Cambridge University Press.

Karpov, Y. (2005). *The Neo-Vygotskian approach to child development.* Cambridge University Press.

Karpov, Y., & Tzuriel, D. (2009). Dynamic assessment: Progress, problems, and prospects. *Journal of Cognitive Education and Psychology, 8*(3), 228–237.

Kern, S. (2003). *The culture of time and space.* Harvard University Press.

Kinard, J., & Kozulin, A. (2008). *Rigorous mathematical thinking: Conceptual formation in the mathematics classroom.* Cambridge University Press.

Kingsbury, G. G., Freeman, E. H., & Nesterak, M. (2014). The potential of adaptive assessment. *Educational Leadership, 71*(6), 12–18.

Klein, P. (2000). A mediational approach to early intervention. In A. Kozulin & Y. Rand (Eds.), *Experience of mediated learning* (pp. 240–256). Pergamon.

Klein, P. S., Wieder, S., & Greenspan, S. I. (1987). A theoretical overview and empirical study of mediated learning experience: Prediction of preschool performance from mother-infant interaction patterns. *Infant Mental Health Journal, 8,* 110–129.

Kozulin, A. (1990). *Vygotsky's psychology: A biography of ideas.* Harvard University Press.

Kozulin, A. (1998). *Psychological tools: A sociocultural approach to education.* Harvard University Press.

Kozulin, A. (2005). Learning potential score as a predictor of sensitivity to cognitive intervention. *Educational and Child Psychology, 22,* 29–39.

Kozulin, A. (2008). Evidence of culture-dependency and modifiability of spatial memory of young adults. *Journal of Cognitive Education and Psychology, 7*(1), 70–80.

Kozulin, A. (2010). Same cognitive performance, different learning potential: Dynamic assessment of young adults with identical cognitive performance. *Journal of Cognitive Education and Psychology, 9*(3), 273–284.

Kozulin, A. (2011) Learning potential and cognitive modifiability. *Assessment in Education: Principles, Policy & Practice, 18*(2), 169–181.

Kozulin, A. (2021). Why teachers need metacognition training? *Cultural-Historical Psychology, 17*(2), 59–64. https://doi.org/10.17759/chp.2021170206.

Kozulin, A., & Garb, E. (2004). Dynamic assessment of literacy: English as a third language. *European Journal of Psychology of Education, 19*, 65–77.

Kuhn, D. (2009). Do students need to be taught how to reason? *Educational Research Review, 4*, 1–6.

Lachman, R., Lachman, J., & Butterfield, E. (2015). *Cognitive psychology and information processing*. Psychology Press.

Lave, J. (1988). *Cognition in practice*. Cambridge University Press.

Leclerc, S. (1637–1714). [Louis XIV Visiting the Royal Academy of Sciences], engraved frontispiece in Claude Perrault (1613–1688), *Memoires pour servir a l'Histoire Naturelle des Animaux* (Paris: Sébastien Mabre-Cramoisy for the Imprimerie royale, 1671–1676).

Lee, J.-E., & Lee, M.-Y. (2018). Tinkering with number line. *Research in Mathematics Education, 21*(1), 1–13.

Lidz, C., & Pena, E. (2009). Response to intervention and dynamic assessment: Do we just appear to be speaking the same language? *Seminars in Speech & Language, 30*(2), 121–133.

Lobato, J., & Ellis, A. (2010). *Developing essential understanding of ratios, proportions, and proportional reasoning for teaching mathematics: Grades 6–8*. National Council of Teachers of Mathematics.

Luria, A. R. (1976). *Cognitive development: Its cultural and social foundations*. Harvard University Press.

Luria, A. R. (1979). *The making of mind*. Harvard University Press.

Marmelshtine, R. (2017). Parent–child learning interactions: A review of the literature on scaffolding. *British Journal of Educational Psychology, 87*(2), 241–254.

Marti, E., & Mayordomo, R. (2003). *How to use a cell phone: Children's and adults' written instructions*. Paper presented at the Conference of the European Association for the Research in Learning and Instruction, Padua, Italy.

Marti, E., Garcia-Mila, M., Gabucio, F., & Konstantinidou, K. (2011). The construction of a double-entry table: A study of primary and secondary school students' difficulties. *European Journal of Psychology of Education, 26*, 215–234.

Martin, M. O., Mullis, I., Gonzalez, E. et al. (1999). *TIMSS 1999 international science report*. Boston College.

Michnick Golinkoff, R., Hoff, E., Rowe, M. L., Tamis-LeMonda, C. S., & Hirsh-Pasek, K. (2019). Language matters: Denying the existence of the 30-Million-Word Gap has serious consequences. *Child Development, 90*(3), 985–992.

Murphy, R., Roschelle, J., Feng, M., & Mason, C. A. (2020). Investigating efficacy, moderators, and mediators for an online mathematics homework intervention. *Journal of Research on Educational Effectiveness, 13*(2), 235–270. https://doi.org/10.1080/19345747.2019.1710885.

Northrup, J., & Iverson, J. (2020). The development of mother–infant coordination across the first year of life. *Developmental Psychology, 56*(2), 221–236.

Ogle, V. (2015). *The global transformation of time.* Harvard University Press.

Olson, D. (1994). *The world on paper: The conceptual and cognitive implications of writing and reading.* Cambridge University Press.

Osiurak, F., Navarro J., & Reynaud, E. (2018). How our cognition shapes and is shaped by technology. *Frontiers in Psychology, 9,* 293. https://doi.org/10.3389/fpsyg.2018.00293.

Otto, B., & Kistner, S. (2017). Is there a Matthew effect in self-regulated learning and mathematical strategy application? – Assessing the effects of a training program with standardized learning diaries. *Learning and Individual Differences, 55,* 75–86.

Pace, A., Alper, R., Burchinal, M. R., Michnick Golinkoff, R., & Hirsh-Pasek, K. (2019). Measuring success: Within and cross-domain predictors of academic and social trajectories in elementary school. *Early Childhood Research Quarterly, 46,* 112–125.

Packiam Alloway, T. (Ed.) (2018). *Working memory and clinical developmental disorders.* Routledge.

Perret-Clermont, A.-N., Perret, J.-F., & Bell, N. (1999). The social construction of meaning and cognitive activity in elementary school children. In P. Lloyd & C. Fernyhough, (Eds.), *Lev Vygotsky: Critical assessments* (vol. 4, pp. 51–73). Routledge.

Piaget, J. (1950). *The psychology of intelligence.* Routledge & Kegan Paul.

PISA. (2000). *Organization for Economic Cooperation and Development.* www.oecd.org/education/school/programmeforinternationalstudentassessmentpisa/publications-pisa2000.htm.

Raven, J. C. (1958). *Standard progressive matrices.* H. K. Lewis.

Rey, A., Feuerstein, R., Jeannet, M., & Richelle, M. (1955). *Quelques aspects de l'état psychologique des enfants juifs marocains.* Rapport (pp. 30–31). Institut des Sciences de l'Education, Université de Genève. [Some aspects of the psychological state of Jewish Moroccan children. Report (pp. 30–31). Institute of the Sciences of Education, University of Geneva.]

Rimskaja, R., & Rimskij, S. (Eds.) (1999). *Practichekaja psychologija v testah* [Practical psychology in tests]. Act-Press.

Rubtsova, O. (2021). Experimenting with roles in adolescence: Applying drama for constructing the zone of proximal development. *Cultural-Historical Psychology, 17*(2), 105–113. https://doi.org/10.17759/chp.2021170210.

Schmittau, J. (2004). Vygotskian theory and mathematics education: Resolving the conceptual-procedural dichotomy. *European Journal of Psychology of Education, 19*(1), 19–43.

Schur, Y., & Kozulin, A. (2008). Cognitive aspects of science problem solving: Two mediated learning experience-based programs. *Journal of Cognitive Education and Psychology, 7*(2), 266–287.

Segall, M. H., Campbell, D. T., & Herskovits, M. J. (1966). *Influence of culture on visual perception.* Bobbs-Merrill.

Sergi, M., Kern, R., Mintz, J., & Green, M. (2005). Learning potential and the prediction of work skill acquisition in schizophrenia. *Schizophrenia Bulletin*, *31*(1), 67–72.

SK-12 Foundation. (2018). *Utah 4th grade science standards*. www.ck12.org.

Spitz, R. (1945). Hospitalism – An Inquiry into the genesis of psychiatric conditions in early childhood. *Psychoanalytic Study of the Child*, *1*, 53–74.

Sternberg, R., & Grigorenko, E. (2002). *Dynamic testing*. Cambridge University Press.

Swartz, R., & McGuinness, C. (2014). *Developing and assessing thinking skills: Final Report Part 1*. https://doi.org/10.13140/RG.2.1.4917.6163.

Swartz, R. J., Costa, A., Kallick, B., Beyer, B., & Reagan, R. (2007). *Thinking-based learning: Activating students' potential*. Christopher-Gordon Publishers.

Thompson, C., Mielicki, M., Rivera, F. et al. (2022). Leveraging math cognition to combat health innumeracy. *Perspectives on Psychological Science*, *20*, 1–26.

Tulsky, D. S., Carlozzi, N. E., Chevalier, N., Espy, K., Beaumont, J., & Mungas, D. (2013). NIH Toolbox Cognitive Function Battery (CFB): Measuring Working Memory. *Society for Research in Child Development, Monograph*, *78*(4), 70–87.

Tzuriel, D. (1996). Mediated learning experience in free-play versus structured situations among preschool children of low-, medium-, and high-SES. *Child Development and Care*, *126*, 57–82.

Tzuriel, D. (1997). The relation between parent-child MLE interactions and children's cognitive modifiability. In A. Kozulin (Ed.), *The Ontogeny of cognitive modifiability* (pp. 157–180). International Center for the Enhancement of Leaning Potential.

Tzuriel, D., & Shamir, A. (2007). The effects of peer-mediation with younger children on children's cognitive modifiability. *British Journal of Educational Psychology*, *77*, 143–165.

van der Veer, R., & Valsiner, J. (1991). *Understanding Vygotsky*. Blackwell.

van Garderen, D., & Montague, M. (2003). Visual–spatial representation, mathematical problem solving, and students of varying abilities. *Learning Disabilities Research & Practice*, *18*, 246–254.

Vaughn, S., Wanzek, J., & Denton, C. A. (2014). Teaching elementary students with learning difficulties. In L. Florian (Ed.), *Handbook of special education* (2nd edn., Vol. 2, pp. 633–657). Sage.

Vosniadou, S. (Ed.) (2008). *International textbook of research on conceptual change*. Routledge.

Vygotsky, L. (1930/1984). Tool and symbol in child behavior. In R. van der Veer & J. Valsiner (Eds.), *The Vygotsky reader* (pp. 99–174). Blackwell.

Vygotsky, L. (1934/2012). *Thought and language*. MIT Press.

Vygotsky, L. (1935/2011). The dynamics of the schoolchild's mental development in relation to teaching and learning. *Journal of Cognitive Education and Psychology*, *10*(2), 198–211.

Vygotsky, L., & Luria, A. R. (1930/1993). *Studies on the history of behavior: Ape, primitive, and child*. Laurence Erlbaum Associates.

Vysotskaya, E., Lobanova, A., Rekhtman, I., & Yanishevskaya, M. (2021). The challenge of proportion: Does it require rethinking of the measurement paradigm? *Educational Studies in Mathematics, 106*, 429–446.

Wang, T.-H. (2011). Implementation of Web-based dynamic assessment in facilitating junior high school students to learn mathematics. *Computers & Education, 56*, 1062–1071.

Weinstein, E., & James, C. (2022). *Behind their screens: What teens are facing (and adults are missing)*. MIT Press.

Wentzel, K., & Watkins, D. (2002). Peer relationships and collaborative learning as contexts for academic enablers. *School Psychology Review, 31*(3), 366–377.

Wood, D., Bruner, J., & Ross, G. (1976). The role of tutoring in problem solving. *Journal of Child Psychology and Psychiatry, 17*(2), 89–100.

Wu, H. M., Kuo, B. C., & Wang, S. C. (2017). Computerized dynamic adaptive tests with immediately individualized feedback for primary school mathematics learning. *Educational Technology & Society, 20*(1), 61–72.

Zohar, A., & Lustov, E. (2018). Challenges in addressing metacognition in professional development programs in the context of instruction of higher-order thinking. In Y. Weinberger & Z. Libman (Eds.), *Contemporary pedagogies in teacher education and development* (pp. 87–100). IntechOpen.

Zuckerman, G. (2004). Development of reflection through learning activity. *European Journal of Psychology of Education, 19*(1), 9–18.

Zuckerman, G. (2007). Child-adult interaction that creates a zone of proximal development. *Journal of Russian & East European Psychology, 45*(3), 43–69.

Zuckerman, G. (2014). Developmental education. In A. Yanitsky, R. van der Veer, & M. Ferrari (Eds.), *The Cambridge handbook of cultural-historical psychology* (pp. 177–202). Cambridge University Press.

Zuckerman, G., & Venger, A. (2010). *Razvitie uchebnoj samostojatel'nosti* [Development of learning independence]. Open Institute for Developing Education.

Zuzovsky, R. (2001). *Achievement of Israeli 8th grade students in TIMSS 1999.* (in Hebrew). Ramot Press.

Zuzovsky, R., & Tamir, P. (1999). Growth patterns in students' ability to supply scientific explanations: Findings from the Third International Mathematics and Science Study in Israel. *International Journal of Science Education, 21*, 1101–1121.

Index

For EU product safety concerns, contact us at Calle de José Abascal, 56–1°,
28003 Madrid, Spain or eugpsr@cambridge.org.

www.ingramcontent.com/pod-product-compliance
Ingram Content Group UK Ltd.
Pitfield, Milton Keynes, MK11 3LW, UK
UKHW020351140625

459647UK00020B/2402